ACHIEVEMENT

ACHIEVEMENT

THE **GREATEST** **BUSINESS MINDS** ON **SUCCESS**

*

J.R.D. Tata, Henry Ford,
Azim Premji and Others

SPEAKING TIGER PUBLISHING PVT. LTD
4381/4, Ansari Road, Daryaganj
New Delhi 110002

Edition copyright © Speaking Tiger 2019

The copyright for the individual pieces vests with the
original authors or their estates

ISBN: 978-93-88326-58-2
eISBN: 978-93-88326-57-5

10 9 8 7 6 5 4 3 2 1

Typeset in Minion Pro by SŪRYA, New Delhi

All rights reserved.
No part of this publication may be reproduced, transmitted,
or stored in a retrieval system, in any form or by any means,
electronic, mechanical, photocopying, recording or otherwise,
without the prior permission of the publisher.

This book is sold subject to the condition that it shall not,
by way of trade or otherwise, be lent, resold, hired out,
or otherwise circulated, without the publisher's
prior consent, in any form of binding
or cover other than that in
which it is published.

'We are kept from our goal not by obstacles, but by a clear path to a lesser goal.'
—The Bhagvad Gita

Contents

Desire: The Starting Point of All Achievement *Napoleon Hill*	9
Take Charge of Your Career Destiny *Azim Premji*	47
My Fundamental Principles of Building and Running a Business *Henry Ford*	53
The Lessons Life Taught Me *Narayana Murthy*	75
Learnings from a Life Well Lived *John D. Rockefeller*	85
Managing the Future *Kiran Mazumdar-Shaw*	101
Persevere *P.T. Barnum*	107
Strive for Perfection and You Will Reach Excellence *J.R.D. Tata*	127

Beat Stress and Adopt Good Working Habits 133
Dale Carnegie

The Perseverence of Ardeshir Godrej 165
B.K. Karanjia

Words of Wisdom to Inspire You 189

Desire: The Starting Point of All Achievement

Napoleon Hill

Napoleon Hill (1883–1970) was a bestselling American author of books like The Law of Success *(1928) and* Think and Grow Rich *(1937), which are still in print today. He interviewed some of the most successful entrepreneurs of his time, including Andrew Carnegie, Henry Ford and Thomas Edison, among others. In the following excerpt from* Think and Grow Rich, *Hill demonstrates through remarkable real-life examples that despite the inevitability of failure, the systematic pursuit of one's dreams forms the core of the entrepreneurial spirit.*

~

The Man Who 'Thought' His Way into Partnership with Thomas A. Edison

Truly, 'thoughts are things', and powerful things at that, when they are mixed with definiteness of purpose, persistence, and a *burning desire* for their translation into riches, or other material objects.

A little more than thirty years ago, Edwin C. Barnes discovered how true it is that men really do *think and grow rich*. His discovery did not come about at one sitting. It came little by little, beginning with a *burning desire* to become a business associate of the great Edison.

One of the chief characteristics of Barnes' Desire was that it was definite. He wanted to work with Edison, not for him. Observe, carefully, the description of how he went about translating his *desire* into reality, and you will have a better understanding of the thirteen principles which lead to riches.

When this *desire,* or impulse of thought, first flashed into his mind he was in no position to act upon it. Two difficulties stood in his way. He did not know Mr Edison, and he did not have enough money to pay his railroad fare to Orange, New Jersey. These difficulties were sufficient to have discouraged the majority of men from making any attempt to carry out the desire.

But his was no ordinary desire! He was so determined to find a way to carry out his desire that he finally decided to travel by 'blind baggage', rather than be defeated. (To the uninitiated, this means that he went to East Orange on a freight train). He presented himself at Mr Edison's laboratory, and announced he had come to go into business with the inventor. In speaking of the first meeting between Barnes and

Edison, years later, Mr Edison said, 'He stood there before me, looking like an ordinary tramp, but there was something in the expression of his face which conveyed the impression that he was determined to get what he had come after. I had learned, from years of experience with men, that when a man really *desires* a thing so deeply that he is willing to stake his entire future on a single turn of the wheel in order to get it, he is sure to win. I gave him the opportunity he asked for, because I saw he had made up his mind to stand by until he succeeded. Subsequent events proved that no mistake was made.'

Just what young Barnes said to Mr Edison on that occasion was far less important than that which he thought. Edison, himself, said so! It could not have been the young man's appearance which got him his start in the Edison office, for that was definitely against him. It was what he *thought* that counted. If the significance of this statement could be conveyed to every person who reads it, there would be no need for the remainder of this book.

Barnes did not get his partnership with Edison on his first interview. He did get a chance to work in the Edison offices, at a very nominal wage, doing work that was unimportant to Edison, but most important to Barnes, because it gave him an opportunity to

Achievement

display his 'merchandise' where his intended 'partner' could see it.

Months went by. Apparently nothing happened to bring the coveted goal which Barnes had set up in his mind as his *definite major purpose*. But something important was happening in Barnes' mind. He was constantly intensifying his *desire* to become the business associate of Edison. Psychologists have correctly said that 'when one is truly ready for a thing, it puts in its appearance.' Barnes was ready for a business association with Edison, moreover, he was *determined to remain ready until he got that which he was seeking.*

He did not say to himself, 'Ah well, what's the use? I guess I'll change my mind and try for a salesman's job.' But, he did say, 'I came here to go into business with Edison, and I'll accomplish this end if it takes the remainder of my life.' He meant it! What a different story men would have to tell if only they would adopt a *definite purpose*, and stand by that purpose until it had time to become an all-consuming obsession!

Maybe young Barnes did not know it at the time, but his bulldog determination, his persistence in standing back of a single *desire*, was destined to mow down all opposition, and bring him the opportunity he was seeking.

When the opportunity came, it appeared in a different form, and from a different direction than Barnes had expected. That is one of the tricks of opportunity. It has a sly habit of slipping in by the back door, and often it comes disguised in the form of misfortune, or temporary defeat. Perhaps this is why so many fail to recognize opportunity.

Mr Edison had just perfected a new office device, known at that time, as the Edison Dictating Machine (now the Ediphone). His salesmen were not enthusiastic over the machine. They did not believe it could be sold without great effort. Barnes saw his opportunity. It had crawled in quietly, hidden in a queer-looking machine which interested no one but Barnes and the inventor.

Barnes knew he could sell the Edison Dictating Machine. He suggested this to Edison, and promptly got his chance. He did sell the machine. In fact, he sold it so successfully that Edison gave him a contract to distribute and market it all over the nation. Out of that business association grew the slogan, 'Made by Edison and installed by Barnes'.

The business alliance has been in operation for more than thirty years. Out of it Barnes has made himself rich in money, but he has done something infinitely greater, he has proved that one really may 'Think and Grow Rich'.

How much actual cash that original *desire* of Barnes' has been worth to him, I have no way of knowing. Perhaps it has brought him two or three million dollars, but the amount, whatever it is, becomes insignificant when compared with the greater asset he acquired in the form of definite knowledge that an intangible impulse of thought can be transmuted into its physical counterpart by the application of known principles.

Barnes literally thought himself into a partnership with the great Edison! He thought himself into a fortune. He had nothing to start with, except the capacity to *know what he wanted, and the determination to stand by that desire until he realized it.* He had no money to begin with. He had but little education. He had no influence. But he did have initiative, faith, and the will to win. With these intangible forces he made himself the number one man with the greatest inventor who ever lived.

The Secret of Henry Ford

Before success comes in any man's life, he is sure to meet with much temporary defeat, and, perhaps, some failure. When defeat overtakes a man, the easiest and most logical thing to do is to *quit*. That is exactly what the majority of men do.

More than five hundred of the most successful men this country has ever known, told the author their greatest success came just one step beyond the point at which defeat had overtaken them. Failure is a trickster with a keen sense of irony and cunning. It takes great delight in tripping one when success is almost within reach.

Millions of people look at the achievements of Henry Ford, after he has arrived, and envy him, because of his good fortune, or luck, or genius, or whatever it is that they credit for Ford's fortune. Perhaps one person in every hundred thousand knows the secret of Ford's success, and those who do know are too modest, or too reluctant, to speak of it, because of its simplicity. A single transaction will illustrate the 'secret' perfectly.

A few years back, Ford decided to produce his now famous V-8 motor. He chose to build an engine with the entire eight cylinders cast in one block, and instructed his engineers to produce a design for the engine. The design was placed on paper, but the engineers agreed, to a man, that it was simply impossible to cast an eight-cylinder gas engine block in one piece.

Ford said, 'Produce it anyway.' 'But,' they replied, 'it's impossible!' 'Go ahead,' Ford commanded, 'and stay on the job until you succeed no matter how much time is required.'

The engineers went ahead. There was nothing else for them to do, if they were to remain on the Ford staff. Six months went by, nothing happened. Another six months passed, and still nothing happened. The engineers tried every conceivable plan to carry out the orders, but the thing seemed out of the question; 'impossible!'

At the end of the year Ford checked with his engineers, and again they informed him they had found no way to carry out his orders.

'Go right ahead,' said Ford, 'I want it, and I'll have it.' They went ahead, and then, as if by a stroke of magic, the secret was discovered.

The Ford *determination* had won once more!

This story may not be described with minute accuracy, but the sum and substance of it is correct. Deduce from it, you who wish to *think and grow rich*, the secret of the Ford millions, if you can. You'll not have to look very far.

Henry Ford is a success, because he understands, and applies the principles of success. One of these is *desire*: knowing what one wants. Remember this Ford story as you read, and pick out the lines in which the secret of his stupendous achievement has been described. If you can do this, if you can lay your finger on the particular group of principles which made Henry Ford rich, you can equal his achievements in almost any calling for which you are suited.

Desire: The Starting Point of All Achievement

The first step toward Riches when Edwin C. Barnes climbed down from the freight train in Orange, N. J., more than thirty years ago, he may have resembled a tramp, but his thoughts were those of a king!

As he made his way from the railroad tracks to Thomas A. Edison's office, his mind was at work. He saw himself standing in Edison's presence. He heard himself asking Mr Edison for an opportunity to carry out the one *consuming obsession of his life*, a *burning desire* to become the business associate of the great inventor.

Barnes' desire was not a hope! It was not a wish! It was a keen, pulsating *desire*, which transcended everything else. It was *definite.*

The desire was not new when he approached Edison. It had been Barnes' dominating desire for a long time. In the beginning, when the desire first appeared in his mind, it may have been, probably was, only a wish, but it was no mere wish when he appeared before Edison with it.

ACHIEVEMENT

A few years later, Edwin C. Barnes again stood before Edison, in the same office where he first met the inventor. This time his *desire* had been translated into reality. He was in business with Edison. The dominating *dream of his life* had become a reality.

Today, people who know Barnes envy him, because of the 'break' life yielded him. They see him in the days of his triumph, without taking the trouble to investigate the cause of his success. Barnes succeeded because he chose a definite goal, placed all his energy, all his will power, all his effort, everything back of that goal. He did not become the partner of Edison the day he arrived. He was content to start in the most menial work, as long as it provided an opportunity to take even one step toward his cherished goal. Five years passed before the chance he had been seeking made its appearance. During all those years not one ray of hope, not one promise of attainment of his *desire* had been held out to him. To everyone, except himself, he appeared only another cog in the Edison business wheel, but in his own mind, *he was the partner of Edison every minute of the time*, from the very day that he first went to work there.

It is a remarkable illustration of the power of a *definite desire*. Barnes won his goal, because he wanted to be a business associate of Mr Edison, more than he wanted anything else. He created a plan by which to attain that purpose. But he *burned all bridges behind him.* He stood by his *desire* until it became the dominating obsession of his life—and—finally, a fact.

When he went to Orange, he did not say to himself, 'I will try to induce Edison to give me a job of some sort.' He said, 'I will see Edison, and put him on notice that I have come to go into business with him. He did not say, 'I will work there for a few months, and if I get no encouragement, I will quit and get a job somewhere else.' He did say, 'I will start anywhere. I will do anything Edison tells me to do, but before I am through, I will be his associate.'

He did not say, 'I will keep my eyes open for another opportunity, in case I fail to get what I want in the Edison organization.' He said, 'There is but *one* thing in this world that I am determined to have, and that is a business association with Thomas A. Edison. I will burn all bridges behind me, and stake my *entire future* on my ability to get what I want.'

He left himself no possible way of retreat. He had to win or perish!

That is all there is to the Barnes story of success! A long while ago, a great warrior faced a situation which made it necessary for him to make a decision which insured his success on the battlefield. He was about to send his armies against a powerful foe, whose men outnumbered his own. He loaded his soldiers into boats, sailed to the enemy's country, unloaded soldiers and equipment, then gave the order to burn the ships that had carried them. Addressing his men before the first battle, he said, 'You see the boats going up in smoke. That means that we cannot leave these shores alive unless we win! We now have no choice—we win—or we perish! They won.

Every person who wins in any undertaking must be willing to burn his ships and cut all sources of retreat. Only by so doing can one be sure of maintaining that state of mind known as a *burning desire to win*, essential to success. The morning after the Great Chicago Fire, a group of merchants stood on State Street, looking at the smoking remains of what had been their stores. They went into a conference to decide if they would try to rebuild, or leave Chicago and start over in a more promising section of the country. They reached a decision—all except one—to leave Chicago.

The merchant who decided to stay and rebuild pointed a finger at the remains of his store, and said, 'Gentlemen, on that very spot I will build the world's greatest store, no matter how many times it may burn down.'

That was more than fifty years ago. The store was built. It stands there today, a towering monument to the power of that state of mind known as a *burning desire*. The easy thing for Marshal Field to have done, would have been exactly what his fellow merchants did. When the going was hard, and the future looked dismal, they pulled up and went where the going seemed easier.

Mark well this difference between Marshal Field and the other merchants, because it is the same difference which distinguishes Edwin C. Barnes from thousands of other young men who have worked in the Edison organization. It is the same difference which distinguishes practically all who succeed from those who fail.

Every human being who reaches the age of understanding of the purpose of money, wishes for it. Wishing will not bring riches. But desiring riches with a state of mind that becomes an obsession, then planning definite ways and means to acquire riches, and backing those plans with persistence which does not recognize failure, will bring riches.

The method by which *desire* for riches can be transmuted into its financial equivalent, consists of six definite, practical steps, viz:

First: Fix in your mind the exact amount of money you desire. It is not sufficient merely to say 'I want plenty of money.' Be definite as to the amount. (There is a psychological reason for definite-ness which will be described in a subsequent chapter).

Second: Determine exactly what you intend to give in return for the money you desire. (There is no such reality as 'something for nothing'.)

Third: Establish a definite date when you intend to possess the money you desire.

Fourth: Create a definite plan for carrying out your desire, and begin at once, whether you are ready or not, to put this plan into action.

Fifth: Write out a clear, concise statement of the amount of money you intend to acquire, name the time limit for its acquisition, state what you intend to give in return for the money, and describe clearly the plan through which you intend to accumulate it.

Sixth: Read your written statement aloud, twice daily, once just before retiring at night, and once after arising in the morning. *As you read—see and feel and believe yourself already in possession of the money.*

It is important that you follow the instructions described in these six steps. It is especially important that you observe, and follow the instructions in the sixth paragraph. You may complain that it is impossible for you to 'see yourself in possession of money' before you actually have it. Here is where a *burning desire* will come to your aid. If you truly *desire* money so keenly that your desire is an obsession, you will have no difficulty in convincing yourself that you will acquire it. The object is to want money, and to become so determined to have it that you *convince* yourself you will have it.

Only those who become 'money conscious' ever accumulate great riches. 'Money consciousness' means that the mind has become so thoroughly saturated with the *desire* for money, that one can see one's self already in possession of it.

To the uninitiated, who has not been schooled in the working principles of the human mind, these instructions may appear impractical. It may be helpful, to all who fail to recognize the soundness of the six steps, to know that the information they convey, was received from Andrew Carnegie, who began as an ordinary labourer in the steel mills, but managed, despite his humble beginning, to make these principles yield him a fortune of considerably more than one hundred million dollars.

It may be of further help to know that the six

steps here recommended were carefully scrutinized by the late Thomas A. Edison, who placed his stamp of approval upon them as being, not only the steps essential for the accumulation of money, but necessary for the attainment of any definite goal.

The steps call for no 'hard labour'. They call for no sacrifice. They do not require one to become ridiculous, or credulous. To apply them calls for no great amount of education. But the successful application of these six steps does call for sufficient imagination to enable one to see, and to understand, that accumulation of money cannot be left to chance, good fortune, and luck. One must realize that all who have accumulated great fortunes, first did a certain amount of dreaming, hoping, wishing, *desiring*, and *planning* before they acquired money.

You may as well know, right here, that you can never have riches in great quantities, *unless* you can work yourself into a white heat of *desire* for money, and actually *believe* you will possess it.

You may as well know, also that every great leader, from the dawn of civilization down to the present, was a dreamer...

Lincoln dreamed of freedom for the black slaves, put his dream into action, and barely missed living to see a united North and South translate his dream into reality.

The Wright brothers dreamed of a machine that would fly through the air. Now one may see evidence all over the world, that they dreamed soundly.

Marconi dreamed of a system for harnessing the intangible forces of the ether. Evidence that he did not dream in vain, may be found in every wireless and radio in the world. Moreover, Marconi's dream brought the humblest cabin, and the most stately manor house side by side. It made the people of every nation on earth back-door neighbours. It gave the President of the United States a medium by which he may talk to all the people of America at one time, and on short notice.

It may interest you to know that Marconi's 'friends' had him taken into custody, and examined in a psychopathic hospital, when he announced he had discovered a principle through which he could send messages through the air, without the aid of wires, or other direct physical means of communication. The dreamers of today fare better.

The world has become accustomed to new discoveries. Nay, it has shown a willingness to reward the dreamer who gives the world a new idea.

'The greatest achievement was, at first, and for a time, but a dream.'

'The oak sleeps in the acorn. The bird waits in the

egg, and in the highest vision of the soul, a waking angel stirs. *Dreams are the seedlings of reality.*

Awake, arise, and assert yourself, you dreamers of the world. Your star is now in the ascendency. The world depression brought the opportunity you have been waiting for. It taught people humility, tolerance, and open-mindedness.

The world is filled with an abundance of *opportunity* which the dreamers of the past never knew.

A burning desire to be, and to do is the starting point from which the dreamer must take off. Dreams are not born of indifference, laziness, or lack of ambition.

The world no longer scoffs at the dreamer, nor calls him impractical. If you think it does, take a trip to Tennessee, and witness what a dreamer President has done in the way of harnessing, and using the great water power of America. A score of years ago, such a dream would have seemed like madness.

You have been disappointed, you have undergone defeat during the depression, you have felt the great heart within you crushed until it bled. Take courage, for these experiences have tempered the spiritual metal of which you are made—they are assets of incomparable value.

Remember, too, that all who succeed in life get off

to a bad start, and pass through many heartbreaking struggles before they 'arrive'. The turning point in the lives of those who succeed, usually comes at the moment of some crisis, through which they are introduced to their 'other selves'.

John Bunyan wrote the *Pilgrim's Progress*, which is among the finest of all English literature, after he had been confined in prison and sorely punished, because of his views on the subject of religion.

O. Henry discovered the genius which slept within his brain, after he had met with great misfortune, and was confined in a prison cell, in Columbus, Ohio. Being *forced*, through misfortune, to become acquainted with his 'other self', and to use his *imagination*, he discovered himself to be a great author instead of a miserable criminal and outcast.

Strange and varied are the ways of life, and stranger still are the ways of Infinite Intelligence, through which men are sometimes forced to undergo all sorts of punishment before discovering their own brains, and their own capacity to create useful ideas through imagination.

Edison, the world's greatest inventor and scientist, was a 'tramp' telegraph operator. He failed innumerable times before he was driven, finally, to the discovery of the genius which slept within his brain.

ACHIEVEMENT

Charles Dickens began by pasting labels on blacking pots. The tragedy of his first love penetrated the depths of his soul, and converted him into one of the world's truly great authors. That tragedy produced, first, *David Copperfield*, then a succession of other works that made this a richer and better world for all who read his books. Disappointment over love affairs, generally has the effect of driving men to drink, and women to ruin; and this, because most people never learn the art of transmuting their strongest emotions into dreams of a constructive nature.

Helen Keller became deaf, dumb, and blind shortly after birth. Despite her greatest misfortune, she has written her name indelibly in the pages of the history of the great. Her entire life has served as evidence that no one ever is defeated until defeat has been accepted as a reality.

Robert Burns was an illiterate country lad, he was cursed by poverty, and grew up to be a drunkard in the bargain. The world was made better for his having lived, because he clothed beautiful thoughts in poetry, and thereby plucked a thorn and planted a rose in its place.

Booker T. Washington was born in slavery, handicapped by race and colour. Because he was tolerant, had an open mind at all times, on all subjects, and was a *dreamer*, he left his impress for good on an entire race.

Beethoven was deaf, Milton was blind, but their names will last as long as time endures, because they dreamed and translated their dreams into organized thought.

Before passing to the next chapter, kindle anew in your mind the fire of hope, faith, courage, and tolerance. If you have these states of mind, and a working knowledge of the principles described, all else that you need will come to you, when you are *ready* for it.

Let Emerson state the thought in these words:

'Every proverb, every book, every byword that belongs to thee for aid and comfort shall surely come home through open or winding passages.

Every friend whom not thy fantastic will, but the great and tender soul in thee craveth, shall lock thee in his embrace.'

There is a difference between *wishing* for a thing and being *ready* to receive it. No one is ready for a thing, until he believes he can acquire it. The state of mind must be *belief*, not mere hope or wish. Open-mindedness is essential for belief.

Closed minds do not inspire faith, courage, and belief. Remember, no more effort is required to aim high in life, to demand abundance and prosperity, than is required to accept misery and poverty. A great poet has correctly stated this universal truth through these lines:

> I bargained with Life for a penny,
> And Life would pay no more,
> However I begged at evening
> When I counted my scanty store.
> For Life is a just employer,
> He gives you what you ask,
> But once you have set the wages,
> Why, you must bear the task.
> I worked for a menial's hire,
> Only to learn, dismayed,
> That any wage I had asked of Life,
> Life would have willingly paid.

Desire Outwits Mother Nature

As a fitting climax to this chapter, I wish to introduce one of the most unusual persons I have ever known. I first saw him twenty-four years ago, a few minutes after he was born. He came into the world without any physical sign of ears, and the doctor admitted, when pressed for an opinion, that the child might be deaf, and mute for life.

I challenged the doctor's opinion. I had the right to do so, I was the child's father.

I, too, reached a decision, and rendered an opinion, but I expressed the opinion silently, in the secrecy of my own heart. I decided that my son would hear and speak. Nature could send me a child without ears, but Nature could not induce me to accept the reality of the affliction.

In my own mind I knew that my son would hear and speak. How? I was sure there must be a way, and I knew I would find it. I thought of the words of the immortal Emerson, 'The whole course of things goes to teach us faith. We need only obey.'

There is guidance for each of us, and by lowly listening, we shall hear the right word.'

The right word? *Desire*! More than anything else, I *desired* that my son should not be a deaf-mute. From that desire I never receded, not for a second.

Many years previously, I had written, 'Our only limitations are those we set up in our own minds.' For the first time, I wondered if that statement were true. Lying on the bed in front of me was a newly born child, without the natural equipment of hearing. Even though he might hear and speak, he was obviously disfigured for life. Surely, this was a limitation which that child had not set up in his own mind.

What could I do about it? Somehow I would find a way to transplant into that child's mind my own *burning desire* for ways and means of conveying sound to his brain without the aid of ears. As soon as the child was old enough to cooperate, I would fill his mind so completely with a *burning desire* to hear, that Nature would, by methods of her own, translate it into physical reality.

All this thinking took place in my own mind, but I spoke of it to no one. Every day I renewed the pledge I had made to myself: not to accept a deaf-mute for a son.

As he grew older, and began to take notice of things around him, we observed that he had a slight degree of hearing. When he reached the age when children usually begin talking, he made no attempt to speak, but we could tell by his actions that he could hear certain sounds slightly. That was all I wanted to know! I was convinced that if he could hear, even slightly, he might develop still greater hearing capacity. Then something happened which gave me hope. It came from an entirely unexpected source.

We bought a victrola. When the child heard the music for the first time, he went into ecstasies, and promptly appropriated the machine. He soon showed a preference for certain records, among them, 'It's a Long Way to Tipperary'. On one occasion, he played that piece over and over, for almost two hours, standing in front of the victrola, with his teeth clamped on the edge of the case. The significance of this self-formed habit of his did not become clear to us until years afterward, for we had never heard of the principle of 'bone conduction' of sound at that time.

Shortly after he appropriated the victrola, I discovered that he could hear me quite clearly when I spoke with my lips touching his mastoid bone, or at the base of the brain. These discoveries placed in my possession the necessary media by which I began to translate into reality my Burning Desire to help my son develop hearing and speech. By that time he was making stabs at speaking certain words.

The outlook was far from encouraging, but *desire backed by faith* knows no such word as impossible.

Having determined that he could hear the sound of my voice plainly, I began, immediately, to transfer to his mind the desire to hear and speak. I soon discovered that the child enjoyed bedtime stories, so I went to work, creating stories designed to develop in him self-reliance, imagination, and a keen desire to hear and to be normal.

There was one story in particular, which I emphasized by giving it some new and dramatic colouring each time it was told. It was designed to plant in his mind the thought that his affliction was

Achievement

not a liability, but an asset of great value. Despite the fact that all the philosophy I had examined clearly indicated that *every adversity brings with it the seed of an equivalent advantage,* I must confess that I had not the slightest idea how this affliction could ever become an asset. However, I continued my practice of wrapping that philosophy in bedtime stories, hoping the time would come when he would find some plan by which his handicap could be made to serve some useful purpose.

Reason told me plainly, that there was no adequate compensation for the lack of ears and natural hearing equipment.

Desire backed by *faith*, pushed reason aside, and inspired me to carry on. As I analyze the experience in retrospect, I can see now, that my son's faith in me had much to do with the astounding results.

He did not question anything I told him. I sold him the idea that he had a distinct advantage over his older brother, and that this advantage would reflect itself in many ways. For example, the teachers in school would observe that he had no ears, and, because of this, they would show him special attention and treat him with extraordinary kindness. They always did. His mother saw to that, by visiting the teachers and arranging with them to give the child the extra attention necessary. I sold him the idea, too, that when he became old enough to sell newspapers (his older brother had already become a newspaper merchant), he would have a big advantage over his brother, for the reason that people would pay him extra money for his wares, because they could see that he was a bright, industrious boy, despite the fact he had no ears.

We could notice that, gradually, the child's hearing was improving. Moreover, he had not the slightest tendency to be self-conscious, because of his affliction. When he was about seven, he showed the first evidence that our method of servicing his mind was bearing fruit. For several months he begged for the privilege of selling newspapers, but his mother would not give her consent. She was afraid that his deafness made it unsafe for him to go on the street alone.

Finally, he took matters in his own hands. One afternoon, when he was left at home with the servants, he climbed through the kitchen window, shinnied to the ground, and set out on his own. He borrowed six cents in capital from the neighbourhood shoemaker, invested it in papers, sold out, reinvested, and kept repeating until late in the evening. After balancing his accounts, and paying back the six cents he had borrowed from his banker, he had a net profit of forty-two cents.

When we got home that night, we found him in bed asleep, with the money tightly clenched in his hand. His mother opened his hand, removed the coins, and cried. Of all things! Crying over her son's first victory seemed so inappropriate. My reaction was the reverse.

I laughed heartily, for I knew that my endeavour to plant in the child's mind an attitude of faith in himself had been successful.

His mother saw, in his first business venture, a little deaf boy who had gone out in the streets and risked his life to earn money. I saw a brave, ambitious, self-reliant little business man whose stock in himself had been increased a hundred per cent, because he had gone into business on his own initiative, and had won.

The transaction pleased me, because I knew that he had given evidence of a trait of resourcefulness that would go with him all through life.

Later events proved this to be true. When his older brother wanted something, he would lie down on the floor, kick his feet in the air, cry for it—and get it. When the 'little deaf boy' wanted something, he would plan a way to earn the money, then buy it for himself. He still follows that plan!

Truly, my own son has taught me that handicaps can be converted into stepping stones on which one may climb toward some worthy goal, unless they are accepted as obstacles, and used as alibis.

The little deaf boy went through the grades, high school, and college without being able to hear his teachers, excepting when they shouted loudly, at close range. He did not go to a school for the deaf. *We would not permit him to learn the sign language.* We were determined that he should live a normal life, and associate with normal children, and we stood by that decision, although it cost us many heated debates with school officials.

While he was in high school, he tried an electrical hearing-aid, but it was of no value to him; due, we believed, to a condition that was disclosed when the child was six, by Dr J. Gordon Wilson, of Chicago, when he operated on one side of the boy's head, and discovered that there was no sign of natural hearing equipment.

During his last week in college, (eighteen years after the operation), something happened which marked the most important turning-point of his life. Through what seemed to be mere chance, he came into possession of another electrical hearing device, which was sent to him on trial. He was slow about testing it, due to his disappointment with a similar device. Finally he picked the instrument up, and more or less carelessly, placed it on his head, hooked up the battery, and lo! as if by a stroke of magic, his lifelong *desire for normal hearing became a reality*! For the first time in his life he heard practically as well as any person with normal hearing.

'God moves in mysterious ways, His wonders to perform.'

Overjoyed because of the Changed World which had been brought to him through his hearing device, he rushed to the telephone, called his mother, and heard her voice perfectly. The next day he plainly heard the voices of his professors in class, for the first time in his life! Previously he could hear them only when they shouted, at short range. He heard the radio. He heard the talking pictures. For the first time in his life, he could converse freely with other people, without the necessity of their having to speak loudly. Truly, he had come into possession of a Changed World. We had refused to accept Nature's error, and, by *persistent desire*, we had induced Nature to correct that error, through the only practical means available.

Desire had commenced to pay dividends, but the victory was not yet complete.

The boy still had to find a definite and practical way to convert his handicap into an equivalent asset. Hardly realizing the significance of what had already been accomplished, but intoxicated with the joy of his newly discovered world of sound, he wrote a letter to the manufacturer of the hearing-aid, enthusiastically describing his experience.

Something in his letter; something, perhaps which was not written on the lines, but back of them; caused the company to invite him to New York. When he arrived, he was escorted through the factory, and while talking with the Chief Engineer, telling him about his changed world, a hunch, an idea, or an inspiration—call it what you wish—flashed into his mind. It was this impulse of thought which converted his affliction into an asset, destined to pay dividends in both money and happiness to thousands for all time to come.

The sum and substance of that impulse of thought was this: It occurred to him that he might be of help to the millions of deafened people who go through life without the benefit of hearing devices, if he could find a way to tell them the story of his Changed World.

Then and there, he reached a decision to devote the remainder of his life to rendering useful service to the hard of hearing. For an entire month, he carried on an intensive research, during which he analyzed the entire marketing system of the manufacturer of the hearing device, and created ways and means of communicating with the hard of hearing all over the

ACHIEVEMENT

world for the purpose of sharing with them his newly discovered 'Changed World'. When this was done, he put in writing a two-year plan, based upon his findings. When he presented the plan to the company, he was instantly given a position, for the purpose of carrying out his ambition.

Little did he dream, when he went to work, that he was destined to bring hope and practical relief to thousands of deafened people who, without his help, would have been doomed forever to deaf-mutism.

Shortly after he became associated with the manufacturer of his hearing aid, he invited me to attend a class conducted by his company, for the purpose of teaching deaf-mutes to hear, and to speak. I had never heard of such a form of education, therefore I visited the class, skeptical but hopeful that my time would not be entirely wasted. Here I saw a demonstration which gave me a greatly enlarged vision of what I had done to arouse and keep alive in my son's mind the *desire* for normal hearing. I saw deaf-mutes actually being taught to hear and to speak, through application of the self-same principle I had used, more than twenty years previously, in saving my son from deaf-mutism.

Thus, through some strange turn of the Wheel of Fate, my son, Blair, and I have been destined to aid in correcting deaf-mutism for those as yet unborn, because we are the only living human beings, as far as I know, who have established definitely the fact that deaf-mutism can be corrected to the extent of restoring to normal life those who suffer with this affliction. It has been done for one; it will be done for others.

There is no doubt in my mind that Blair would have been a deaf-mute all his life, if his mother and I had not managed to shape his mind as we did. The doctor who attended at his birth told us, confidentially, the child might never hear or speak.

A few weeks ago, Dr Irving Voorhees, a noted specialist on such cases, examined Blair very thoroughly. He was astounded when he learned how well my son now hears, and speaks, and said his examination indicated that 'theoretically, the boy should not be able to hear at all.' But the lad does hear, despite the fact that X-ray pictures show there is no opening in the skull, whatsoever, from where his ears should be to the brain.

When I planted in his mind the *desire* to hear and talk, and live as a normal person, there went with that impulse some strange influence which caused Nature to become bridge-builder, and span the gulf of silence between his brain and the outer world, by some means which the keenest medical specialists have not been able to interpret. It would be sacrilege for me to even conjecture as to how Nature performed this miracle. It would be unforgivable if I neglected to tell the world as much as I know of the humble part I assumed in the strange experience.

It is my duty, and a privilege to say I believe, and not without reason, that nothing is impossible to the person who backs *desire* with enduring *faith*.

Verily, a *burning desire* has devious ways of transmuting itself into its physical equivalent. Blair *desired* normal hearing; now he has it! He was born with a handicap which might easily have sent one with a less defined *desire* to the street with a bundle of pencils and a tin cup. That handicap now promises to serve as the medium by which he will render useful service to many millions of hard of hearing, also, to give him useful employment at adequate financial compensation the remainder of his life.

The little 'white lies' I planted in his mind when he was a child, by leading him to *believe* his affliction would become a great asset, which he could capitalize, has justified itself. Verily, there is nothing, right or wrong, which *belief*, plus *burning desire*, cannot make real. These qualities are free to everyone. In all my experience in dealing with men and women who had personal problems, I never handled a single case which more definitely demonstrates the power of *desire*. Authors sometimes make the mistake of writing of subjects of which they have but superficial, or very elementary knowledge. It has been my good fortune to have had the privilege of testing the soundness of the *power of desire*, through the affliction of my own son. Perhaps it was providential that the experience came as it did, for surely no one is better prepared than he, to serve as an example of what happens when *desire* is put to the test. If Mother Nature bends to the will of desire, is it logical that mere men can defeat a burning desire?

Strange and imponderable is the power of the human mind! We do not understand the method by which it uses every circumstance, every individual, every physical thing within its reach, as a means of transmuting *desire* into its physical counterpart. Perhaps science will uncover this secret. I planted in my son's mind the *desire* to hear and to speak as any normal person hears and speaks.

That *desire* has now become a reality. I planted in his mind the *desire* to convert his greatest handicap into his greatest asset. That *desire* has been realized.

The modus operandi by which this astounding result was achieved is not hard to describe. It consisted of three very definite facts; first, I mixed *faith* with the *desire* for normal hearing, which I passed on to my son. Second, I communicated my desire to him in every conceivable way available, through persistent, continuous effort, over a period of years. Third, *he believed me*!

As this chapter was being completed, news came of the death of Mme. Schuman-Heink. One short paragraph in the news dispatch gives the clue to this unusual woman's stupendous success as a singer. I quote the paragraph, because the clue it contains is none other than *desire*.

> Early in her career, Mme. Schuman-Heink visited the director of the Vienna Court Opera, to have him test her voice. But, he did not test it. After taking one look at the awkward and poorly dressed girl, he exclaimed, none too gently, 'With such a face, and with no personality at all, how can you ever expect to succeed in opera? My good child, give up the idea. Buy a sewing machine, and go to work. *You can never be a singer.*

Never is a long time! The director of the Vienna Court Opera knew much about the technique of singing. He knew little about the power of desire, when it assumes the proportion of an obsession. If he had known more of that power, he would not have made the mistake of condemning genius without giving it an opportunity.

Several years ago, one of my business associates became ill. He became worse as time went on, and finally was taken to the hospital for an operation.

Just before he was wheeled into the operating room, I took a look at him, and wondered how anyone as thin and emaciated as he, could possibly go through a major operation successfully. The doctor warned me that there was little if any chance of my ever seeing him alive again. But that was the *doctor's opinion*. It was not the opinion of the patient. Just before he was wheeled away, he whispered feebly, 'Do not be disturbed, Chief, I will be out of here in a few days.' The attending nurse looked at me with pity. But the patient did come through safely.

After it was all over, his physician said, 'Nothing but his own desire to live saved him. He never would have pulled through if he had not refused to accept the possibility of death.'

I believe in the power of *desire* backed by *faith*, because I have seen this power lift men from lowly beginnings to places of power and wealth; I have seen it rob the grave of its victims; I have seen it serve as the medium by which men staged a comeback after having been defeated in a hundred different ways; I have seen it provide my own son with a normal, happy, successful life, despite Nature's having sent him into the world without ears.

ACHIEVEMENT

How can one harness and use the power of *desire*? This has been answered through this, and the subsequent chapters of this book. This message is going out to the world at the end of the longest, and perhaps, the most devastating depression America has ever known. It is reasonable to presume that the message may come to the attention of many who have been wounded by the depression, those who have lost their fortunes, others who have lost their positions, and great numbers who must reorganize their plans and stage a comeback. To all these I wish to convey the thought that all achievement, no matter what may be its nature, or its purpose, must begin with an intense, *burning desire* for something definite.

Through some strange and powerful principle of 'mental chemistry' which she has never divulged, Nature wraps up in the impulse of *strong desire* 'that something' which recognizes no such word as impossible, and accepts no such reality as failure.

Take Charge of Your Career Destiny

Azim Premji

Azim Premji is a leading business tycoon, investor and philanthropist. As Chairman, Wipro Limited, he is informally known as the Czar of the Indian IT industry. He guided Wipro through four decades of diversification and growth to become a global leader in the software industry. In the following speech delivered on 12 August, 2016, Premji shares the importance of following your inner voice, earning through your own labour, being open to failure, sticking with your core values and giving back to the society which has nurtured our endeavours.

~

The funny thing about life is that you realize the value of something only when it begins to leave you. As my hair turned from black to salt and pepper and finally salt without the pepper, I have begun to realize the enthusiasm and excitement of youth.

At the same time, I have begun to truly appreciate some of the lessons I have learnt along the way. As you embark on your careers, I would like to share them with you. I am hoping that you will find them as useful as I have.

Achievement

The world you are entering is in many ways very different now from what it was when I began my career. It was the late sixties and India still depended on other countries for something as basic as food. We aroused sympathy, not admiration whenever we went overseas. Recently, someone told me, that when visitors came to India then, they came to see what they could do for India. Now, they come to see what India can do for them. As a hopeful Indian, I look at our country as one which is rich in ethnic and cultural diversity and one that has an effective, secular democracy which will help us build an enduring society.

Lesson 1: Take Charge

This was the first thought that came to me when over four decades ago, I stepped into the Wipro factory at Amalner. I was twenty-one and had spent the last few years in Stanford University Engineering School at California. Many people advised me to take up a nice, cushy job rather than face the challenges of running a hydrogenated oil business. Looking back, I am glad I decided to take charge instead. Essentially, leadership begins from within. It is a small voice that tells you where to go when you feel lost. If you believe in that voice, you believe in yourself. When it comes to choosing your careers, you have to take charge of your own destiny.

Lesson 2: Earn Your Happiness

The second lesson I have learnt is that a rupee earned is of far more value than five found. In fact, what is gifted or inherited follows the old rule of come easy, go easy. I guess we only know the value of what we have if we have struggled to earn it.

Lesson 3: Nothing Succeeds Like Failure

The third lesson I have learnt is no one bats a hundred every time. Life has many challenges. You win some and lose some. You must enjoy winning. But do not let it go to the head. The moment it does, you are already on your way to failure. And if you do encounter failure along the way, treat it as an equally natural phenomenon. The important thing is, when you lose, do not lose the lesson.

Lesson 4: Nothing Fails Like Success

The fourth lesson I have learnt is the importance of humility. There is a thin line of difference between confidence and arrogance. Confident people are always open to learn. A recent survey of executives in Europe showed that the single most important quality needed for leadership success was the willingness to learn from any situation. Arrogance on the other hand stops learning. It comes with a feeling that one knows all that needs to be known and has done all that needs to be done.

Lesson 5: There Has to be a Better Way

Partly as a corollary to what I have just said, we must remember that no matter how well we do something there has to be a better way! Excellence is not a destination but a journey. Creativity and innovation sometimes need inspiration from other disciplines. It is probably not a chance that Einstein's interest in music was as much as his interest in Physics. Bertrand Russell was as much a mathematician as a philosopher. Excellence and creativity go hand in hand.

Lesson 6: Respond, Not React

There is a world of difference between the two and in terms of success and failure. The difference is that the mind comes in between responding and reacting. When we respond, we evaluate with a calm mind and do whatever is most appropriate. We are in control of our actions. When we react, we are still doing what the other person wants us to do.

Lesson 7: Remain Physically Active

It is easy to take health for granted when you are young. I have found that exercise not only improves the quality of time but also reduces the time you need for sleep. The truth is that stress will only increase in a global world. You must have your own mechanism to deal with it.

Lesson 8: Never Compromise on Your Core Values

Mahatma Gandhiji often said that you must open the windows of your mind, but you must not be swept off your feet by the breeze. One must define what you stand for. This is not difficult. But values lie, not in the words used to describe them, as much as in the simple acts. And that is the hard part. Like someone said, 'I could not hear what you said because what you did was coming out far too loud.'

Lesson 9: Play to Win

Playing to win brings out the best in us and in our teams. It brings out the desire to stretch, to achieve that which seems beyond our grasp. However, it is not about winning at any cost. It is not about winning every time. It is not about winning at the expense of others. It is about innovating all the time. It is a continuous endeavour to do better than last time.

Lesson 10: Give Back to Society

All of us have a collective social responsibility towards doing our bit to address them. Of all the challenges, the key to me is education. We have a paradoxical situation, where on the one hand we have jobs chasing scarce talent and on the other, rampant unemployment and poverty. The only way to bridge these two ends of the pole is by providing quality education that is accessible by all.

My Fundamental Principles of Building and Running a Business

Henry Ford

Henry Ford (1863-1947) was an American business magnate and the founder of the Ford Motor Company, which not only took the automobile to the masses, but also ensured that it was affordable and dependable. In this excerpt from his autobiography, My Life and My Work *(1922), Ford narrates his journey from giving up a cushy, but limiting, job at the Edison Electrical Company to pursuing his dream of building an affordable motor vehicle. One of the greatest learnings on his entrepreneurial journey was the revelation that the most successful businesses are those which focus on providing good quality products and customer service rather than those which look to the 'immediate dollar'. Ford laid down not only the blueprint for the modern mass-production as we know it, but also taught that fixating solely on profit brings not only on a fear of failure, but also hampers our capacity to change with the times.*

~

My 'gasoline buggy' was the first and for a long time the only automobile in Detroit. It was considered to be something of a nuisance, for it made a racket and it scared horses. Also it blocked traffic. For if I stopped my machine anywhere in town a crowd was around it before I could start up again. If I left it alone even for a minute some inquisitive person always tried to run it. Finally, I had to carry a chain and chain it to a lamp post whenever I left it anywhere. And then there was trouble with the police. I do not know quite why, for my impression is that there were no speed-limit laws in those days. Anyway, I had to get a special permit from the mayor and thus for a time enjoyed the distinction of being the only licensed chauffeur in America. I ran that machine about one thousand miles through 1895 and 1896 and then sold it to Charles Ainsley of Detroit for two hundred dollars. That was my first sale. I had built the car not to sell but only to experiment with. I wanted to start another car. Ainsley wanted to buy. I could use the money and we had no trouble in agreeing upon a price.

It was not at all my idea to make cars in any such petty fashion. I was looking ahead to production, but before that could come I had to have something to produce. It does not pay to hurry. I started a second car in 1896; it was much like the first but a little lighter. It also had the belt drive which I did not give up until sometime later; the belts were all right excepting in hot weather. That is why I later adopted gears. I learned a great deal from that car. Others in this country and abroad were building cars by that time, and in 1895 I heard that a Benz car from Germany was on exhibition in Macy's store in New York. I traveled down to look at it but it had no features that seemed worthwhile. It also had the belt drive, but it was much heavier than my car. I was working for lightness; the foreign makers have never seemed to appreciate what light weight means. I built three cars in all in my home shop and all of them ran for years in Detroit. I still have the first car; I bought it back a few years later from a man to whom Mr Ainsley had sold it. I paid one hundred dollars for it.

During all this time I kept my position with the electric company and gradually advanced to chief engineer at a salary of one hundred and twenty-five dollars a month. But my gas-engine experiments were no more popular with the president of the company than my first mechanical leanings were with my father. It was not that my employer objected to experiments—only to experiments with a gas engine. I can still hear him say: 'Electricity, yes, that's the coming thing. But gas—no.'

He had ample grounds for his skepticism—to use the mildest terms. Practically no one had the remotest notion of the future of the internal combustion engine, while we were just on the edge of the great electrical development. As with every comparatively new idea, electricity was expected to do much more than we even now have any indication that it can do. I did not see the use of experimenting with electricity for my purposes. A road car could not run on a trolley even if trolley wires had been less expensive; no storage battery was in sight of a weight that was practical. An electrical car had of necessity to be limited in radius and to contain a large amount of motive machinery in proportion to the power exerted. That is not to say that I held or now hold electricity cheaply; we have not yet begun to use electricity. But it has its place, and the internal combustion engine has its place. Neither can substitute for the other—which is exceedingly fortunate.

I have the dynamo that I first had charge of at the Detroit Edison Company. When I started our Canadian plant I bought it from an office building to which it had been sold by the electric company, had it revamped a little, and for several years it gave excellent service in the Canadian plant. When we had to build a new power plant, owing to the increase in business, I had the old motor taken out to my museum—a room out at Dearborn that holds a great number of my mechanical treasures.

The Edison Company offered me the general superintendency of the company but only on condition that I would give up my gas engine and devote myself to something really useful. I had to choose between my job and my automobile. I chose the automobile, or rather I gave up the job—there was really nothing in the way of a choice. For already I knew that the car was bound to be a success. I quit my job on August 15, 1899, and went into the automobile business.

It might be thought something of a step, for I had no personal funds. What money was left over from living was all used in experimenting. But my wife agreed that the automobile could not be given up— that we had to make or break. There was no 'demand' for automobiles—there never is for a new article. They were accepted in much the fashion as was more recently the airplane. At first the 'horseless carriage' was considered merely a freak notion and many wise people explained with particularity why it could never be more than a toy. No man of money even thought of it as a commercial possibility. I cannot imagine why each new means of transportation meets with such opposition. There are even those to-day who shake their heads and talk about the luxury of the automobile and only grudgingly admit that perhaps the motor truck is of some use. But in the beginning there was

Achievement

hardly any one who sensed that the automobile could be a large factor in industry. The most optimistic hoped only for a development akin to that of the bicycle. When it was found that an automobile really could go and several makers started to put out cars, the immediate query was as to which would go fastest. It was a curious but natural development—that racing idea. I never thought anything of racing, but the public refused to consider the automobile in any light other than as a fast toy. Therefore later we had to race. The industry was held back by this initial racing slant, for the attention of the makers was diverted to making fast rather than good cars. It was a business for speculators.

A group of men of speculative turn of mind organized, as soon as I left the electric company, the Detroit Automobile Company to exploit my car. I was the chief engineer and held a small amount of the stock. For three years we continued making cars more or less on the model of my first car. We sold very few of them; I could get no support at all toward making better cars to be sold to the public at large. The whole thought was to make to order and to get the largest price possible for each car. The main idea seemed to be to get the money. And being without authority other than my engineering position gave me, I found that the new company was not a vehicle for realizing my ideas but merely a money-making concern—that did not make much money. In March, 1902, I resigned, determined never again to put myself under orders. The Detroit Automobile Company later became the Cadillac Company under the ownership of the Lelands, who came in subsequently.

I rented a shop—a one-story brick shed—at 81 Park Place to continue my experiments and to find out what business really was. I thought that it must be something different from what it had proved to be in my first adventure.

The year from 1902 until the formation of the Ford Motor Company was practically one of investigation. In my little one-room brick shop I worked on the development of a four-cylinder motor and on the outside I tried to find out what business really was and whether it needed to be quite so selfish a scramble for money as it seemed to be from my first short experience. From the period of the first car, which I have described, until the formation of my present company I built in all about twenty-five cars, of which nineteen or twenty were built with the Detroit Automobile Company. The automobile had passed from the initial stage where the fact that it could run at all was enough, to the stage where it had to show speed. Alexander Winton of Cleveland, the founder of the Winton car, was then the track champion of the country and willing to meet all comers. I designed a two-cylinder enclosed engine of a more compact type than I had before used, fitted it into a skeleton chassis, found that I could make speed, and arranged a race with Winton. We met on the Grosse Point track at Detroit. I beat him. That was my first race, and it brought advertising of the only kind that people cared to read. The public thought nothing of a car unless it made speed—unless it beat other racing cars. My ambition to build the fastest car in the world led me to plan a four-cylinder motor. But of that more later.

The most surprising feature of business as it was conducted was the large attention given to finance and the small attention to service. That seemed to me to be reversing the natural process which is that the money should come as the result of work and not before the work. The second feature was the general indifference to better methods of manufacture as long as whatever was done got by and took the money. In other words, an article apparently was not built with reference to how greatly it could serve the public but with reference solely to how much money could be had for it—and that without any particular care whether the customer was satisfied. To sell him was enough. A dissatisfied customer was regarded not as a man whose trust had been violated, but either as a nuisance or as a possible source of more money in fixing up the work which ought to have been done correctly in the first place. For instance, in automobiles there was not much concern as to what happened to the car once it had been sold. How much gasoline it used per mile was of no great moment; how much service it actually gave did not matter; and if it broke down and had to have parts replaced, then that was just hard luck for the owner. It was considered good business to sell parts at the highest possible price on the theory that, since the man had already bought the car, he simply had to have the part and would be willing to pay for it.

The automobile business was not on what I would call an honest basis, to say nothing of being, from a manufacturing standpoint, on a scientific basis, but it was no worse than business in general. That was the period, it may be remembered, in which many corporations were being floated and financed. The bankers, who before then had confined themselves to the railroads, got into industry. My idea was then and still is that if a man did his work well, the price he would get for that work, the profits and all financial matters, would care for themselves and that a business ought to start small and build itself up and out of its earnings. If there are no earnings then that is a signal to the owner that he is wasting his time and does not belong in that business. I have never found it necessary to change those ideas, but I discovered that this simple formula of doing good work and getting paid for it was supposed to be slow for modern business. The plan at that time most in favor was to start off with the largest possible capitalization and then sell all the stock and all the bonds that could be sold. Whatever money happened to be left over after all the stock and bond-selling expenses and promoters, charges and all that, went grudgingly into the foundation of the business. A good business was not one that did good work and earned a fair profit. A good business was one that would give the opportunity for the floating of a large amount of stocks and bonds at high prices. It was the stocks and bonds, not the work, that mattered. I could not see how a new business or an old business could be expected to be able to charge into its product a great big bond interest and then sell the product at a fair price. I have never been able to see that.

I have never been able to understand on what theory the original investment of money can be charged against a business. Those men in business who call themselves financiers say that money is 'worth' 6 per cent, or 5 per cent, or some other per cent, and that if a business has one hundred thousand dollars invested in it, the man who made the investment is entitled to charge an interest payment on the money, because, if instead of putting that money into the business he had put it into a savings bank or into certain securities, he could have a certain fixed return. Therefore they say that a proper charge against the operating expenses of a business is the interest on this money. This idea is at the root of many business failures and most service failures. Money is not worth a particular amount. As money it is not worth anything, for it will do nothing of itself. The only use of money is to buy tools to work with or the product of tools. Therefore money is worth what it will help you to produce or buy and no more. If a man thinks that his money will earn 5 per cent, or 6 per cent, he ought to place it where he can get that return, but money placed in a business is not a charge on the business—or, rather, should not be. It ceases to be money and becomes, or should become, an engine of production, and it is therefore worth what it produces—and not a fixed sum according to some scale that has no bearing upon the particular business in which the money has been placed. Any return should come after it has produced, not before.

Business men believed that you could do anything by 'financing' it. If it did not go through on the first financing then the idea was to 'refinance'. The process

Achievement

of 'refinancing' was simply the game of sending good money after bad. In the majority of cases the need of refinancing arises from bad management, and the effect of refinancing is simply to pay the poor managers to keep up their bad management a little longer. It is merely a postponement of the day of judgment. This makeshift of refinancing is a device of speculative financiers. Their money is no good to them unless they can connect it up with a place where real work is being done, and that they cannot do unless, somehow, that place is poorly managed. Thus, the speculative financiers delude themselves that they are putting their money out to use. They are not; they are putting it out to waste.

I determined absolutely that never would I join a company in which finance came before the work or in which bankers or financiers had a part. And further that, if there were no way to get started in the kind of business that I thought could be managed in the interest of the public, then I simply would not get started at all. For my own short experience, together with what I saw going on around me, was quite enough proof that business as a mere money-making game was not worth giving much thought to and was distinctly no place for a man who wanted to accomplish anything. Also it did not seem to me to be the way to make money. I have yet to have it demonstrated that it is the way. For the only foundation of real business is service.

A manufacturer is not through with his customer when a sale is completed. He has then only started with his customer. In the case of an automobile the sale of the machine is only something in the nature of an introduction. If the machine does not give service, then it is better for the manufacturer if he never had the introduction, for he will have the worst of all advertisements—a dissatisfied customer. There was something more than a tendency in the early days of the automobile to regard the selling of a machine as the real accomplishment and that thereafter it did not matter what happened to the buyer. That is the shortsighted salesman-on-commission attitude. If a salesman is paid only for what he sells, it is not to be expected that he is going to exert any great effort on a customer out of whom no more commission is to be made. And it is right on this point that we later made the largest selling argument for the Ford. The price and the quality of the car would undoubtedly have made a market, and a large market. We went beyond that. A man who bought one of our cars was in my opinion entitled to continuous use of that car, and therefore if he had a breakdown of any kind it was

Achievement

our duty to see that his machine was put into shape again at the earliest possible moment. In the success of the Ford car the early provision of service was an outstanding element. Most of the expensive cars of that period were ill provided with service stations. If your car broke down you had to depend on the local repair man—when you were entitled to depend upon the manufacturer. If the local repair man were a forehanded sort of a person, keeping on hand a good stock of parts (although on many of the cars the parts were not interchangeable), the owner was lucky. But if the repair man were a shiftless person, with an adequate knowledge of automobiles and an inordinate desire to make a good thing out of every car that came into his place for repairs, then even a slight breakdown meant weeks of laying up and a whopping big repair bill that had to be paid before the car could be taken away. The repair men were for a time the largest menace to the automobile industry. Even as late as 1910 and 1911 the owner of an automobile was regarded as essentially a rich man whose money ought to be taken away from him. We met that situation squarely and at the very beginning. We would not have our distribution blocked by stupid, greedy men.

That is getting some years ahead of the story, but it is control by finance that breaks up service because it looks to the immediate dollar. If the first consideration is to earn a certain amount of money, then, unless by some stroke of luck matters are going especially well and there is a surplus over for service so that the operating men may have a chance, future business has to be sacrificed for the dollar of to-day.

And also I noticed a tendency among many men in business to feel that their lot was hard—they worked against a day when they might retire and live on an income—get out of the strife. Life to them was a battle to be ended as soon as possible. That was another point I could not understand, for as I reasoned, life is not a battle except with our own tendency to sag with the downpull of 'getting settled'. If to petrify is success all one has to do is to humour the lazy side of the mind but if to grow is success, then one must wake up anew every morning and keep awake all day. I saw great businesses become but the ghost of a name because someone thought they could be managed just as they were always managed, and though the management may have been most excellent in its day, its excellence consisted in its alertness to its day, and not in slavish following of its yesterdays. Life, as I see it, is not a location, but a journey. Even the man who most feels himself 'settled' is not settled—he is probably sagging back. Everything is in flux, and was meant to be. Life flows. We may live at the same number of the street, but it is never the same man who lives there.

And out of the delusion that life is a battle that may be lost by a false move grows, I have noticed, a great love for regularity. Men fall into the half-alive habit. Seldom does the cobbler take up with the new-fangled way of soling shoes, and seldom does the artisan willingly take up with new methods in his trade. Habit conduces to a certain inertia, and any disturbance of it affects the mind like trouble. It will be recalled that when a study was made of shop methods, so that the workmen might be taught to produce with less useless motion and fatigue, it was most opposed by the workmen themselves. Though they suspected that it was simply a game to get more out of them, what most irked them was that it interfered with the well-worn grooves in which they had become accustomed to move. Business men go down with their businesses because they like the old way so well they cannot bring themselves to change. One sees them all about—men who do not know that yesterday is past, and who woke up this morning with their last year's ideas. It could almost be written down as a formula that when a man begins to think that he has at last found his method he had better begin a most searching examination of himself to see whether some part of his brain has not gone to sleep. There is a subtle danger in a man thinking that he is 'fixed' for life. It indicates that the next jolt of the wheel of progress is going to fling him off.

There is also the great fear of being thought a fool. So many men are afraid of being considered fools. I grant that public opinion is a powerful police influence for those who need it. Perhaps it is true that the majority of men need the restraint of public opinion. Public opinion may keep a man better than he would otherwise be—if not better morally, at least better as far as his social desirability is concerned. But it is not a bad thing to be a fool for righteousness' sake. The best of it is that such fools usually live long enough to prove that they were not fools—or the work they have begun lives long enough to prove they were not foolish.

The money influence—the pressing need to make a profit on an 'investment'—and its consequent neglect of or skimping of work and hence of service showed itself to me in many ways. It seemed to be at the bottom of most troubles. It was the cause of low wages—for without well-directed work high wages cannot be paid. And if the whole attention is not given to the work it cannot be well directed. Most men want to be free to work; under the system in use they

Achievement

could not be free to work. During my first experience I was not free—I could not give full play to my ideas. Everything had to be planned to make money; the last consideration was the work. And the most curious part of it all was the insistence that it was the money and not the work that counted. It did not seem to strike any one as illogical that money should be put ahead of work—even though everyone had to admit that the profit had to come from the work. The desire seemed to be to find a short cut to money and to pass over the obvious short cut—which is through the work.

Take competition; I found that competition was supposed to be a menace and that a good manager circumvented his competitors by getting a monopoly through artificial means. The idea was that there were only a certain number of people who could buy and that it was necessary to get their trade ahead of someone else. Some will remember that later many of the automobile manufacturers entered into an association under the Selden Patent just so that it might be legally possible to control the price and the output of automobiles. They had the same idea that so many trades unions have—the ridiculous notion that more profit can be had doing less work than more. The plan, I believe, is a very antiquated one. I could not see then and am still unable to see that there is not always enough for the man who does his work; time spent in fighting competition is wasted; it had better be spent in doing the work. There are always enough people ready and anxious to buy, provided you supply what they want and at the proper price—and this applies to personal services as well as to goods.

During this time of reflection I was far from idle. We were going ahead with a four-cylinder motor and the building of a pair of big racing cars. I had plenty of time, for I never left my business. I do not believe a man can ever leave his business. He ought to think of it by day and dream of it by night. It is nice to plan to do one's work in office hours, to take up the work in the morning, to drop it in the evening—and not have a care until the next morning. It is perfectly possible to do that if one is so constituted as to be willing through all of his life to accept direction, to be an employee, possibly a responsible employee, but not a director or manager of anything. A manual labourer must have a limit on his hours, otherwise he will wear himself out. If he intends to remain always a manual labourer, then he should forget about his work when the whistle blows, but if he intends to go forward and do anything, the whistle is only a signal to start thinking over the day's work in order to discover how it might be done better.

Achievement

The man who has the largest capacity for work and thought is the man who is bound to succeed. I cannot pretend to say, because I do not know, whether the man who works always, who never leaves his business, who is absolutely intent upon getting ahead, and who therefore does get ahead—is happier than the man who keeps office hours, both for his brain and his hands. It is not necessary for any one to decide the question. A ten-horsepower engine will not pull as much as a twenty. The man who keeps brain office hours limits his horsepower. If he is satisfied to pull only the load that he has, well and good, that is his affair—but he must not complain if another who has increased his horsepower pulls more than he does. Leisure and work bring different results. If a man wants leisure and gets it—then he has no cause to complain. But he cannot have both leisure and the results of work.

Concretely, what I most realized about business in that year—and I have been learning more each year without finding it necessary to change my first conclusions—is this:

1. That finance is given a place ahead of work and therefore tends to kill the work and destroy the fundamental of service.
2. That thinking first of money instead of work

brings on fear of failure and this fear blocks every avenue of business—it makes a man afraid of competition, of changing his methods, or of doing anything which might change his condition.

3. That the way is clear for any one who thinks first of service—of doing the work in the best possible way.

The Lessons Life Taught Me

Narayana Murthy

Narayana Murthy, co-founder of Infosys, and one of the great entrepreneurs of contemporary India, is considered to be the 'father of the Indian IT sector'. The following speech was a pre-commencement lecture delivered at the Stern School of Business, New York University, on 9 May, 2007. In it, Murthy describes his formative experiences as an entrepreneur, learning from failure, and the importance of self-belief and creating value for society at large.

~

After some thought, I have decided to share with you some of my life lessons. I learned these lessons in the context of my early career struggles, a life lived under the influence of sometimes unplanned events which were the crucibles that tempered my character and reshaped my future.

I would like first to share some of these key life events with you, in the hope that these may help you understand my struggles and how chance events and unplanned encounters with influential persons shaped my life and career.

Later, I will share the deeper life lessons that I have

learned. My sincere hope is that this sharing will help you see your own trials and tribulations for the hidden blessings they can be.

The first event occurred when I was a graduate student in Control Theory at IIT, Kanpur, in India. At breakfast on a bright Sunday morning in 1968, I had a chance encounter with a famous computer scientist on sabbatical from a well-known US university.

He was discussing exciting new developments in the field of computer science with a large group of students and how such developments would alter our future. He was articulate, passionate and quite convincing. I was hooked. I went straight from breakfast to the library, read four or five papers he had suggested, and left the library determined to study computer science.

Friends, when I look back today at that pivotal meeting, I marvel at how one role model can alter for the better the future of a young student. This experience taught me that valuable advice can sometimes come from an unexpected source, and chance events can sometimes open new doors.

The next event that left an indelible mark on me occurred in 1974. The location: Nis, a border town between former Yugoslavia, now Serbia, and Bulgaria. I was hitchhiking from Paris back to Mysore, India, my home town.

By the time a kind driver dropped me at Nis railway station at 9 p.m. on a Saturday night, the restaurant was closed. So was the bank the next morning, and I could not eat because I had no local money. I slept on the railway platform until 8.30 p.m. in the night when the Sofia Express pulled in.

The only passengers in my compartment were a girl and a boy. I struck up a conversation in French with the young girl. She talked about the travails of living in an Iron Curtain country, until we were roughly interrupted by some policemen who, I later gathered, were summoned by the young man who thought we were criticizing the Communist government of Bulgaria.

The girl was led away; my backpack and sleeping bag were confiscated. I was dragged along the platform into a small 8x8 foot room with a cold stone floor and a hole in one corner by way of toilet facilities. I was held in that bitterly cold room without food or water for over 72 hours.

I had lost all hope of ever seeing the outside world again when the door opened. I was again dragged out unceremoniously, locked up in the guard's compartment on a departing freight train and told that I would be released 20 hours later upon reaching Istanbul. The guard's final words still ring in my ears—'You are from a friendly country called India and that is why we are letting you go!'

The journey to Istanbul was lonely, and I was starving. This long, lonely, cold journey forced me to deeply rethink my convictions about Communism. Early on a dark Thursday morning, after being hungry for 108 hours, I was purged of any last vestiges of affinity for the Left.

I concluded that entrepreneurship, resulting in large-scale job creation, was the only viable mechanism for eradicating poverty in societies.

Deep in my heart, I always thank the Bulgarian guards for transforming me from a confused Leftist into a determined, compassionate capitalist! Inevitably, this sequence of events led to the eventual founding of Infosys in 1981.

While these first two events were rather fortuitous, the next two, both concerning the Infosys journey, were more planned and profoundly influenced my career trajectory.

On a chilly Saturday morning in the winter of 1990, five of the seven founders of Infosys met in our small office in a leafy Bangalore suburb. The decision at hand was the possible sale of Infosys for the enticing sum of $1 million. After nine years of toil in the then business-unfriendly India, we were quite happy at the prospect of seeing at least some money.

I let my younger colleagues talk about their future plans. Discussions about the travails of our journey thus far and our future challenges went on for about four hours. I had not yet spoken a word.

Finally, it was my turn. I spoke about our journey from a small Mumbai apartment in 1981 that had been beset with many challenges, but also of how I believed we were at the darkest hour before the dawn. I then took an audacious step. If they were all bent upon selling the company, I said, I would buy out all my colleagues, though I did not have a cent in my pocket.

There was a stunned silence in the room. My colleagues wondered aloud about my foolhardiness. But I remained silent. However, after an hour of my arguments, my colleagues changed their minds to my way of thinking. I urged them that if we wanted to create a great company, we should be optimistic and confident. They have more than lived up to their promise of that day.

In the seventeen years since that day, Infosys has grown to revenues in excess of $3.0 billion, a net income of more than $800 million and a market capitalization of more than $28 billion, 28,000 times richer than the offer of $1 million on that day.

In the process, Infosys has created more than 70,000 well-paying jobs, 2,000-plus dollar-millionaires and 20,000-plus rupee millionaires.

Achievement

A final story: On a hot summer morning in 1995, a Fortune 10 corporation had sequestered all their Indian software vendors, including Infosys, in different rooms at the Taj Residency hotel in Bangalore so that the vendors could not communicate with one another. This customer's propensity for tough negotiations was well known. Our team was very nervous.

First of all, with revenues of only around $5 million, we were minnows compared to the customer.

Second, this customer contributed fully 25% of our revenues. The loss of this business would potentially devastate our recently listed company.

Third, the customer's negotiation style was very aggressive. The customer team would go from room to room, get the best terms out of each vendor and then pit one vendor against the other. This went on for several rounds. Our various arguments why a fair price—one that allowed us to invest in good people, R&D, infrastructure, technology and training—was actually in their interest failed to cut any ice with the customer.

By 5 p.m. on the last day, we had to make a decision right on the spot whether to accept the customer's terms or to walk out.

All eyes were on me as I mulled over the decision. I closed my eyes and reflected upon our journey until then. Through many a tough call, we had always thought about the long-term interests of Infosys. I communicated clearly to the customer team that we could not accept their terms, since it could well lead us to letting them down later. But I promised a smooth, professional transition to a vendor of customer's choice.

This was a turning point for Infosys.

Subsequently, we created a Risk Mitigation Council which ensured that we would never again depend too much on any one client, technology, country, application area or key employee. The crisis was a blessing in disguise. Today, Infosys has a sound de-risking strategy that has stabilized its revenues and profits.

I want to share with you, next, the life lessons these events have taught me:

1. I will begin with the importance of learning from experience. It is less important, I believe, where you start. It is more important how and what you learn. If the quality of the learning is high, the development gradient is steep, and, given time, you can find yourself in a previously unattainable place. I believe the Infosys story is living proof of this. Learning

from experience, however, can be complicated. It can be much more difficult to learn from success than from failure. If we fail, we think carefully about the precise cause. Success can indiscriminately reinforce all our prior actions.

2. A second theme concerns the power of chance events. As I think across a wide variety of settings in my life, I am struck by the incredible role played by the interplay of chance events with intentional choices. While the turning points themselves are indeed often fortuitous, how we respond to them is anything but so. It is this very quality of how we respond systematically to chance events that is crucial.

3. Of course, the mindset one works with is also quite critical. As recent work by the psychologist, Carol Dweck, has shown, it matters greatly whether one believes in ability as inherent or something which can be developed. Put simply, the former view, a fixed mindset, creates a tendency to avoid challenges, to ignore useful negative feedback and leads such people to plateau early and not achieve their full potential. The latter view, a growth mindset, leads to a tendency to embrace challenges, to learn from criticism and such

people reach ever higher levels of achievement (Krakovsky, 2007, 48).

4. The fourth theme is a cornerstone of the Indian spiritual tradition: self-knowledge. Indeed, the highest form of knowledge, it is said, is self-knowledge. I believe this greater awareness and knowledge of oneself is what ultimately helps develop a more grounded belief in oneself, courage, determination, and, above all, humility, all qualities which enable one to wear one's success with dignity and grace.

Based on my life experiences, I can assert that it is this belief in learning from experience, a growth mindset, the power of chance events, and self-reflection that have helped me grow to the present.

Back in the 1960s, the odds of my being in front of you today would have been zero. Yet here I stand before you! With every successive step, the odds kept changing in my favour, and it is these life lessons that made all the difference.

My young friends, I would like to end with some words of advice. Do you believe that your future is pre-ordained, and is already set? Or, do you believe that your future is yet to be written and that it will depend upon sometimes fortuitous events?

ACHIEVEMENT

Do you believe that these events can provide turning points to which you will respond with your energy and enthusiasm? Do you believe that you will learn from these events and that you will reflect on your setbacks? Do you believe that you will examine your successes with even greater care?

I hope you believe that the future will be shaped by several turning points with great learning opportunities. In fact, this is the path I have walked to much advantage.

A final word: When, one day, you have made your mark on the world, remember that, in the ultimate analysis, we are all mere temporary custodians of the wealth we generate, whether it be financial, intellectual, or emotional. The best use of all your wealth is to share it with those less fortunate.

I believe that we have all at some time eaten the fruit from trees that we did not plant. In the fullness of time, when it is our turn to give, it behooves us in turn to plant gardens that we may never eat the fruit of, which will largely benefit generations to come. I believe this is our sacred responsibility, one that I hope you will shoulder in time.

Learnings from a Life Well Lived

John D. Rockefeller

John Davison Rockefeller Sr. (1839–1937) was an American oil industry business magnate, industrialist and philanthropist. He is widely considered to be the richest person in modern history. In the following extract from his memoir Random Reminiscences of Men and Events *(1909), Rockefeller stresses the importance of learning from those with experience, sticking to sound business principles, conducting your affairs within the law and taking care of your employees—the timeless mantras for definitive entrepreneurial success.*

~

Work for Your Start, and Make the Most of It

Although the plan had been to send me to college, it seemed best at sixteen that I should leave the high school in which I had nearly completed the course and go into a commercial college in Cleveland for a few months. They taught bookkeeping and some of the fundamental principles of commercial transactions. This training, though it lasted only a few months, was very valuable to me. But how to get a job—that was the question. I tramped the streets for days and

Achievement

weeks, asking merchants and storekeepers if they didn't want a boy; but the offer of my services met with little appreciation. No one wanted a boy, and very few showed any overwhelming anxiety to talk with me on the subject. At last one man on the Cleveland docks told me that I might come back after the noonday meal. I was elated; it now seemed that I might get a start.

I was in a fever of anxiety lest I should lose this one opportunity that I had unearthed. When finally at what seemed to me the time, I presented myself to my would-be employer:

'We will give you a chance,' he said, but not a word passed between us about pay. This was September 26, 1855. I joyfully went to work. The name of the firm was Hewitt & Tuttle.

In beginning the work I had some advantages. My father's training…was practical, the course at the commercial college had taught me the rudiments of business, and I thus had a groundwork to build upon. I was fortunate, also, in working under the supervision of the bookkeeper, who was a fine disciplinarian, and well disposed toward me.

When January, 1856, arrived, Mr Tuttle presented me with $50 for my three months' work, which was no doubt all that I was worth, and it was entirely satisfactory.

For the next year, with $25 a month, I kept my position, learning the details and clerical work connected with such a business. It was a wholesale produce commission and forwarding concern, my department being particularly the office duties. Just above me was the bookkeeper for the house, and he received $2,000 a year salary in lieu of his share of the profits of the firm of which he was a member. At the end of the first fiscal year when he left I assumed his clerical and bookkeeping work, for which I received the salary of $500.

As I look back upon this term of business apprenticeship, I can see that its influence was vitally important in its relations to what came after.

To begin with, my work was done in the office of the firm itself. I was almost always present when they talked of their affairs, laid out their plans, and decided upon a course of action. I thus had an advantage over other boys of my age, who were quicker and who could figure and write better than I. The firm conducted a business with so many ramifications that this education was quite extensive. They owned dwelling-houses, warehouses, and buildings which were rented for offices and a variety of uses, and I had to collect the rents. They shipped by rail, canal, and lake. There were many different kinds of negotiations and transactions going on, and with all these I was in close touch.

Thus it happened that my duties were vastly more interesting than those of an office-boy in a large house to-day. I thoroughly enjoyed the work. Gradually the auditing of accounts was left in my hands. All the bills were first passed upon by me, and I took this duty very seriously.

One day, I remember, I was in a neighbour's office, when the local plumber presented himself with a bill about a yard long. This neighbour was one of those very busy men. He was connected with what seemed to me an unlimited number of enterprises. He merely glanced at this tiresome bill, turned to the bookkeeper, and said:

'Please pay this bill.'

As I was studying the same plumber's bills in great detail, checking every item, if only for a few cents, and finding it to be greatly to the firm's interest to do so, this casual way of conducting affairs did not appeal to me. I had trained myself to the point of view doubtless held by many young men in business to-day, that my check on a bill was the executive act which released my employer's money from the till and was attended with more responsibility than the spending of my own funds. I made up my mind that such business methods could not succeed.

Passing bills, collecting rents, adjusting claims, and work of this kind brought me in association with a great variety of people. I had to learn how to get on with all these different classes, and still keep the relations between them and the house pleasant. One particular kind of negotiation came to me which took all the skill I could master to bring to a successful end.

We would receive, for example, a shipment of marble from Vermont to Cleveland. This involved handling by railroad, canal, and lake boats. The cost of losses or damage had to be somehow fixed between these three different carriers, and it taxed all the ingenuity of a boy of seventeen to work out this problem to the satisfaction of all concerned, including my employers. But I thought the task no hardship, and so far as I can remember I never had any disagreement of moment with any of these transportation interests. This experience in conducting all sorts of transactions at such an impressionable age, with the helping hand of my superiors to fall back upon in an emergency—was highly interesting to me. It was my first step in learning the principle of negotiation…

The training that comes from working for someone else, to whom we feel a responsibility, I am sure was of great value to me.

Achievement

Stay Alert to New Opportunities

...The next year I was offered a salary of $700, but thought I was worth $800. We had not settled the matter by April, and as a favourable opportunity had presented itself for carrying on the same business on my own account, I resigned my position.

In those days, in Cleveland, everyone knew almost everyone else in town. Among the merchants was a young Englishman named M.B. Clark, perhaps ten years older than I, who wanted to establish a business and was in search of a partner. He had $2,000 to contribute to the firm, and wanted a partner who could furnish an equal amount. This seemed a good opportunity for me. I had saved up $700 or $800, but where to get the rest was a problem.

I talked the matter over with my father, who told me that he had always intended to give $1,000 to each of his children when they reached twenty-one. He said that if I wished to receive my share at once, instead of waiting, he would advance it to me and I could pay interest upon the sum until I was twenty-one.

'But, John,' he added, 'the rate is ten.'

At that time, 10 per cent a year interest was a very common rate for such loans. At the banks the rate might not have been quite so high; but of course the financial institutions could not supply all the demands, so there was much private borrowing at high figures. As I needed this money for the partnership, I gladly accepted my father's offer, and so began business as the junior partner of the new firm, which was called Clark & Rockefeller.

It was a great thing to be my own employer. Mentally I swelled with pride—a partner in a firm with $4,000 capital! Mr Clark attended to the buying and selling, and I took charge of the finance and the books. We at once began to do a large business, dealing in carload lots and cargoes of produce. Naturally we soon needed more money to take care of the increasing trade. There was nothing to do but to attempt to borrow from a bank. But would the bank lend to us?

∼

I went to a bank president whom I knew, and who knew me. I remember perfectly how anxious I was to get that loan and to establish myself favourably with the banker. This gentleman was T.P. Handy, a sweet and gentle old man, well known as a high-grade, beautiful character. For fifty years he was interested in young men. He knew me as a boy in the Cleveland schools. I gave him all the particulars of our business, telling him frankly about our affairs—what we wanted to use the money for, etc., etc. I waited for the verdict with almost trembling eagerness.

'How much do you want?' he said.

'Two thousand dollars.'

'All right, Mr Rockefeller, you can have it,' he replied. 'Just give me your own warehouse receipts; they're good enough for me.'

As I left that bank, my elation can hardly be imagined. I held up my head—think of it, a bank had trusted me for $2,000! I felt that I was now a man of importance in the community.

~

Mr Handy trusted me because he believed we would conduct our young business on conservative and proper lines, and I well remember about this time an example of how hard it is sometimes to live up to what one knows is the right business principle. Not long after our concern was started our best customer—that is, the man who made the largest consignments—asked that we should allow him to draw in advance on current shipments before the produce or a bill of lading were actually in hand. We, of course, wished to oblige this important man, but I, as the financial member of the firm, objected, though I feared we should lose his business.

John D. Rockefeller

The situation seemed very serious; my partner was impatient with me for refusing to yield, and in this dilemma I decided to go personally to see if I could not induce our customer to relent. I had been unusually fortunate when I came face to face with men in winning their friendship, and my partner's displeasure put me on my mettle. I felt that when I got into touch with this gentleman I could convince him that what he proposed would result in a bad precedent. My reasoning (in my own mind) was logical and convincing. I went to see him, and put forth all the arguments that I had so carefully thought out. But he stormed about, and in the end I had the further humiliation of confessing to my partner that I had failed. I had been able to accomplish absolutely nothing.

Naturally, he was very much disturbed at the possibility of losing our most valued connection, but I insisted and we stuck to our principles and refused to give the shipper the accommodation he had asked. What was our surprise and gratification to find that he continued his relations with us as though nothing had happened, and did not again refer to the matter. I learned afterward that an old country banker, named John Gardener, of Norwalk, O., who had much to do with our consignor, was watching this little matter

Achievement

intently, and I have ever since believed that he originated the suggestion to tempt us to do what we stated we did not do as a test, and his story about our firm stand for what we regarded as sound business principles did us great good.

About this time I began to go out and solicit business—a branch of work I had never before attempted. I undertook to visit every person in our part of the country who was in any way connected with the kind of business that we were engaged in, and went pretty well over the states of Ohio and Indiana. I made up my mind that I could do this best by simply introducing our firm, and not pressing for immediate consignments. I told them that I represented Clark & Rockefeller, commission merchants, and that I had no wish to interfere with any connection that they had at present, but if the opportunity offered we should be glad to serve them, etc., etc.

To our great surprise, business came in upon us so fast that we hardly knew how to take care of it, and in the first year our sales amounted to half a million dollars.

Then, and indeed for many years after, it seemed as though there was no end to the money needed to carry on and develop the business. As our successes began to come, I seldom put my head upon the pillow at night without speaking a few words to myself in this wise:

'Now a little success, soon you will fall down, soon you will be overthrown. Because you have got a start, you think you are quite a merchant; look out, or you will lose your head—go steady.' These intimate conversations with myself, I am sure, had a great influence on my life. I was afraid I could not stand my prosperity, and tried to teach myself not to get puffed up with any foolish notions.

My loans from my father were many. Our relations on finances were a source of some anxiety to me, and were not quite so humorous as they seem now as I look back at them. Occasionally he would come to me and say that if I needed money in the business he would be able to loan some, and as I always needed capital I was glad indeed to get it, even at 10 per cent interest. Just at the moment when I required the money most he was apt to say:

'My son, I find I have got to have that money.'

'Of course, you shall have it at once,' I would answer, but I knew that he was testing me, and that when I paid him, he would hold the money without its earning anything for a little time, and then offer it back later…

Stick to Fundamental Principles

The underlying, essential element of success in business affairs is to follow the established laws of high-class dealing. Keep to broad and sure lines, and study them to be certain that they are correct ones. Watch the natural operations of trade, and keep within them. Don't even think of temporary or sharp advantages. Don't waste your effort on a thing which ends in a petty triumph unless you are satisfied with a life of petty success. Be sure that before you go into an enterprise you see your way clear to stay through to a successful end. Look ahead. It is surprising how many bright business men go into important undertakings with little or no study of the controlling conditions they risk their all upon.

Study diligently your capital requirements, and fortify yourself fully to cover possible set-backs, because you can absolutely count on meeting set-backs. Be sure that you are not deceiving yourself at any time about actual conditions. The man who starts out simply with the idea of getting rich won't succeed; you must have a larger ambition. There is no mystery in business success. The great industrial leaders have told again and again the plain and obvious fact that there can be no permanent success without fair dealing that leads to wide-spread confidence in the man himself, and that is the real capital we all prize and work for. If you do each day's task successfully, and stay faithfully within these natural operations of commercial laws which I talk so much about, and keep your head clear, you will come out all right, and will then, perhaps, forgive me for moralizing in this old-fashioned way. It is hardly necessary to caution a young man who reads so sober a book as this not to lose his head over a little success, or to grow impatient or discouraged by a little failure.

Learn the Art of Giving Back

I am sure it is a mistake to assume that the possession of money in great abundance necessarily brings happiness. The very rich are just like all the rest of us; and if they get pleasure from the possession of money, it comes from their ability to do things which give satisfaction to someone besides themselves.

The mere expenditure of money for things, so I am told by those who profess to know, soon palls upon one. The novelty of being able to purchase anything one wants soon passes, because what people most seek cannot be bought with money. These rich men we read about in the newspapers cannot get personal returns beyond a well-defined limit for their expenditure. They cannot gratify the pleasures of the palate beyond very moderate bounds, since they cannot purchase a good digestion; they cannot lavish very much money on fine raiment for themselves or their families without suffering from public ridicule; and in their homes they cannot go much beyond the comforts of the less wealthy without involving them in more pain than pleasure. As I study wealthy men, I can see but one way in which they can secure a real equivalent for money spent, and that is to cultivate a taste for giving where the money may produce an effect which will be a lasting gratification.

A man of business may often most properly consider that he does his share in building up a property which gives steady work for few or many people; and his contribution consists in giving to his employees good working conditions, new opportunities, and a strong stimulus to good work. Just so long as he has the welfare of his employees in his mind and follows his convictions, no one can help honouring such a man. It would be the narrowest sort of view to take, and I think the meanest, to consider that good works consist chiefly in the outright giving of money.

The best philanthropy, the help that does the most good and the least harm, the help that nourishes civilization at its very root, that most widely disseminates health, righteousness, and happiness, is not what is usually called charity. It is, in my judgment, the investment of effort or time or money, carefully considered with relation to the power of employing people at a remunerative wage, to expand and develop the resources at hand, and to give opportunity for progress and healthful labour where it did not exist before. No mere money-giving is comparable to this in its lasting and beneficial results.

If I were to give advice to a young man starting out in life, I should say to him: If you aim for a large, broad-gauged success, do not begin your business career, whether you sell your labour or are an independent producer, with the idea of getting from the world by hook or crook all you can. In the choice of your profession or your business employment, let your first thought be: Where can I fit in so that I may be most effective in the work of the world? Where can I lend a hand in a way most effectively to advance the general interests? Enter life in such a spirit, choose your vocation in that way, and you have taken the first step on the highest road to a large success. Investigation will show that the great fortunes which have been made in this country, and the same is probably true of other lands, have come to men who have performed great and far-reaching economic services—men who, with great faith in the future of their country, have done most for the development of its resources. The man will be most successful who confers the greatest service on the world. Commercial enterprises that are needed by the public will pay. Commercial enterprises that are not needed fail, and ought to fail.

We must always remember that there is not enough money for the work of human uplift and that there never can be. How vitally important it is, therefore, that the expenditure should go as far as possible and be used with the greatest intelligence!

Managing the Future

Kiran Mazumdar-Shaw

Kiran Mazumdar-Shaw is the CMD, Biocon Limited, a pioneering Indian biotechnology company. Ms Shaw started Biocon from the garage of her rented house in Bengaluru in 1978, with a seed capital of Rs 10,000. Last year, it crossed sales of more than $1 billion. In the following excerpt from her convocation speech delivered at the Institute of Management Technology, Hyderabad, in March 2018, Ms Shaw discusses her own difficulties in starting out as a young woman entrepreneur, the failures which spurred her on, the importance of a long-term vision, and addressing the environmental and health problems of our country.

~

Failure and Success

As students of management, you would have learned that failure is inherent to building success and am sure you have been coached on managing risk and failure.

In my life's journey, my ability to face and learn from failure helped me a great deal. When I started off as a 25-year-old woman entrepreneur with no business experience and limited financial resources, I had to face huge credibility and perception challenges, as well as, failures. In those days, women were not perceived as good entrepreneurs and biotechnology was unheard of as an industry. The prevailing business ethos favoured low-risk ventures based on services and generic drugs and was averse to risk-ridden, innovation-led businesses like biotechnology. I succeeded against these odds because I understood that all challenges can be surmounted with perseverance and ingenuity.

When you fail, learn from it instead of getting defeated and giving up permanently. My underlying belief is 'Persevere till you succeed. Failure is temporary but giving up is permanent!'

Sense of Purpose

Great companies and great leaders are driven by a deep sense of purpose. Elon Musk is driven by a mission to reduce global warming through sustainable energy production and consumption thereby reducing the risk of human extinction. Bill and Melinda Gates established their foundation on the belief that every life has equal value and have therefore focused their efforts to help all people lead healthy, productive lives by eradicating the world of infectious diseases, hunger and poverty.

My own company, Biocon, is on a mission to make a difference to global health by providing affordable access to life-saving drugs for diabetes and cancer.

I have always believed that Blockbuster drugs are not about a billion dollars but about a billion patients. I would urge all of you to believe in your goals and aspirations and attain them with a sense of purpose.

Success is an Endurance Race

Every one of us faces periods of fatigue, lack of job satisfaction and even serious doubts about whether it is worth pursuing one's efforts. Endurance is the name of the game and those who endure come out stronger and more confident to rise to greater challenges and greater heights.

Far too many young people are lured by the temptation to switch jobs to make an extra buck or to escape work-related stress, and data will tell you that these job-hoppers never make meaningful impact as they fail to develop both experience and expertise.

Overcome Obstacles

Every career path is fraught with obstacles but overcoming obstacles is a confidence-building exercise. My own entrepreneurial journey has been an obstacle race, which I have successfully overcome time and time again to build confidence, quell scepticism and drive leadership. This must also be your resolve as you step into your life's journey.

Achievement

In the words of Michael Jordan, one of the greatest basketball players of all time: 'Obstacles don't have to stop you. If you run into a wall, don't turn around and give up. Figure out how to climb it, or work around it.'

Values and Ethics

There will come a time when you will need to have long-term, strategic goals. Your responsibilities will shift from being task- and activity-oriented to problem gauging and problem solving. This will call for strategic thinking that will enable you to create enduring value for you and the organizations that you serve. This is what builds great companies and great leaders. Integral to this is an uncompromising code of values and ethics.

As the saying goes: 'Ethics is knowing the difference between what you have a right to do and what is right to do...'

True Leaders Spot Opportunity in Challenges

Challenges, I believe, contain the seeds of opportunity, which in turn give birth to innovation and progress. When one is driven by the spirit of leadership, such challenges become milestones on the path to success.

True leaders can come from any walk of life and they are visionaries with a sense of purpose, who persevere and have a passion for change. They know that leadership is not about control but about being able to inspire people with values and vision.

You must channelize the innate leadership instinct that all of us possess and try to make a difference in your own lives as well as in the lives of others. This will not only result in self-empowerment but also help society prosper.

Create Value for Your Country

Today, India needs all of us—especially capable young people like you—to be responsible and address the myriad challenges our country faces: food security, health security, job security, energy security and environmental sustainability.

Remember, our country cannot aspire to economic greatness as long as India remains home to one-fourth of the world's poor and more than one-third of all malnourished children.

So I would like to ask you to get involved and convert these challenges into opportunities that can help bring about transformational change in alleviating human suffering while creating wealth and prosperity for all.

As the leaders of tomorrow, I urge you to go out and pursue your career paths with a spirit of challenge and a deep sense of purpose.

Achievement

Remember, the purposeful pursuit of your passion is the only thing that will ultimately bring fulfilment as you look back at the trajectory of your life. As you venture forth into the world today, I will leave you with one simple advice: Don't just follow your dreams, pursue them purposefully!

Persevere

P.T. Barnum

Phineas Taylor Barnum (1810–1891) was a renowned American showman, author, publisher and businessman. He founded the Barnum & Bailey Circus which ran from 1871 to 2017, and changed the face of the entertainment business. In this excerpt from his book Art of Money Getting *(1880), Barnum lays down the fundamentals of any pursuit in life: choosing the field of your interest and passion, single-mindedly pursuing it, getting your hands dirty and letting your experience guide you to make the important decisions.*

~

Don't Mistake Your Vocation

The safest plan, and the one most sure of success for the young man starting in life, is to select the vocation which is most congenial to his tastes. Parents and guardians are often quite too negligent in regard to this. It very common for a father to say, for example: 'I have five boys. I will make Billy a clergyman; John a lawyer; Tom a doctor, and Dick a farmer.' He then goes into town and looks about to see what he will do with Sammy. He returns home and says, 'Sammy, I see watch-making is a nice genteel business; I think

Achievement

I will make you a goldsmith.' He does this, regardless of Sam's natural inclinations, or genius.

We are all, no doubt, born for a wise purpose. There is as much diversity in our brains as in our countenances. Some are born natural mechanics, while some have great aversion to machinery. Let a dozen boys of ten years get together, and you will soon observe two or three are 'whittling' out some ingenious device; working with locks or complicated machinery. When they were but five years old, their father could find no toy to please them like a puzzle. They are natural mechanics; but the other eight or nine boys have different aptitudes. I belong to the latter class; I never had the slightest love for mechanism; on the contrary, I have a sort of abhorrence for complicated machinery. I never had ingenuity enough to whittle a cider tap so it would not leak. I never could make a pen that I could write with, or understand the principle of a steam engine. If a man was to take such a boy as I was, and attempt to make a watchmaker of him, the boy might, after an apprenticeship of five or seven years, be able to take apart and put together a watch; but all through life he would be working uphill and seizing every excuse for leaving his work and idling away his time. Watchmaking is repulsive to him.

Unless a man enters upon the vocation intended

for him by nature, and best suited to his peculiar genius, he cannot succeed. I am glad to believe that the majority of persons do find their right vocation. Yet we see many who have mistaken their calling, from the blacksmith up (or down) to the clergyman. You will see, for instance, that extraordinary linguist the 'learned blacksmith', who ought to have been a teacher of languages; and you may have seen lawyers, doctors and clergymen who were better fitted by nature for the anvil or the lapstone.

Select the Right Location

After securing the right vocation, you must be careful to select the proper location. You may have been cut out for a hotel keeper, and they say it requires a genius to 'know how to keep a hotel'. You might conduct a hotel like clock-work, and provide satisfactorily for five hundred guests every day; yet, if you should locate your house in a small village where there is no railroad communication or public travel, the location would be your ruin. It is equally important that you do not commence business where there are already enough to meet all demands in the same occupation. I remember a case which illustrates this subject. When I was in London in 1858, I was passing down Holborn with an English friend and came to the 'penny shows'. They had immense cartoons outside, portraying the wonderful curiosities to be seen 'all for a penny'. Being a little in the 'show line' myself, I said 'let us go in here'. We soon found ourselves in the presence of the illustrious showman, and he proved to be the sharpest man in that line I had ever met. He told us some extraordinary stories in reference to his bearded ladies, his Albinos, and his Armadillos, which we could hardly believe, but thought it 'better to believe it than look after the proof'. He finally begged to call our attention to some wax statuary, and showed us a lot of the dirtiest and filthiest wax figures imaginable. They looked as if they had not seen water since the Deluge.

'What is there so wonderful about your statuary?' I asked.

'I beg you not to speak so satirically,' he replied, 'Sir, these are not Madam Tussaud's wax figures, all covered with gilt and tinsel and imitation diamonds, and copied from engravings and photographs. Mine, sir, were taken from life. Whenever you look upon one of those figures, you may consider that you are looking upon the living individual.'

Glancing casually at them, I saw one labeled 'Henry VIII', and feeling a little curious upon seeing that it looked like Calvin Edson, the living skeleton, I said: 'Do you call that "Henry the Eighth?"' He replied,

'Certainly, sir; it was taken from life at Hampton Court, by special order of his majesty; on such a day.'

He would have given the hour of the day if I had resisted; I said, 'Everybody knows that "Henry VIII" was a great stout old king, and that figure is lean and lank; what do you say to that?'

'Why,' he replied, 'you would be lean and lank yourself if you sat there as long as he has.'

There was no resisting such arguments. I said to my English friend, 'Let us go out; do not tell him who I am; I show the white feather; he beats me.'

He followed us to the door, and seeing the rabble in the street, he called out, 'Ladies and gentlemen, I beg to draw your attention to the respectable character of my visitors,' pointing to us as we walked away. I called upon him a couple of days afterwards; told him who I was, and said: 'My friend, you are an excellent showman, but you have selected a bad location.'

He replied, 'This is true, sir; I feel that all my talents are thrown away; but what can I do?'

'You can go to America,' I replied. 'You can give full play to your faculties over there; you will find plenty of elbowroom in America; I will engage you for two years; after that you will be able to go on your own account.'

He accepted my offer and remained two years in

my New York Museum. He then went to New Orleans and carried on a traveling show business during the summer. To-day he is worth sixty thousand dollars, simply because he selected the right vocation and also secured the proper location. The old proverb says, 'Three removes are as bad as a fire,' but when a man is in the fire, it matters but little how soon or how often he removes...

Persevere

When a man is in the right path, he must persevere. I speak of this because there are some persons who are 'born tired'; naturally lazy and possessing no self-reliance and no perseverance. But they can cultivate these qualities, as Davy Crockett said:

'This thing remember, when I am dead: Be sure you are right, then go ahead.'

It is this go-aheaditiveness, this determination not to let the 'horrors' or the 'blues' take possession of you, so as to make you relax your energies in the struggle for independence, which you must cultivate.

How many have almost reached the goal of their ambition, but, losing faith in themselves, have relaxed their energies, and the golden prize has been lost forever.

It is, no doubt, often true, as Shakespeare says:

'There is a tide in the affairs of men,
Which, taken at the flood, leads on to fortune.'

If you hesitate, some bolder hand will stretch out before you and get the prize. Remember the proverb of Solomon: 'He becometh poor that dealeth with a slack hand; but the hand of the diligent maketh rich.'

Perseverance is sometimes but another word for self-reliance. Many persons naturally look on the dark side of life, and borrow trouble. They are born so. Then they ask for advice, and they will be governed by one wind and blown by another, and cannot rely upon themselves. Until you can get so that you can rely upon yourself, you need not expect to succeed.

I have known men, personally, who have met with pecuniary reverses, and absolutely committed suicide, because they thought they could never overcome their misfortune. But I have known others who have met more serious financial difficulties, and have bridged them over by simple perseverance, aided by a firm belief that they were doing justly, and that Providence would 'overcome evil with good'. You will see this illustrated in any sphere of life.

Take two generals; both understand military tactics, both educated at West Point, if you please, both equally gifted; yet one, having this principle of perseverance, and the other lacking it, the former will succeed in his profession, while the latter will fail. One may hear the cry, 'The enemy are coming, and they have got cannon.'

'Got cannon?' says the hesitating general.

'Yes.'

'Then halt every man.'

He wants time to reflect; his hesitation is his ruin; the enemy passes unmolested, or overwhelms him; while on the other hand, the general of pluck, perseverance and self-reliance, goes into battle with a will, and, amid the clash of arms, the booming of cannon, the shrieks of the wounded, and the moans of the dying, you will see this man persevering, going on, cutting and slashing his way through with unwavering determination, inspiring his soldiers to deeds of fortitude, valor, and triumph.

Whatever You Do, Do It With All Your Might

Work at it, if necessary, early and late, in season and out of season, not leaving a stone unturned, and never deferring for a single hour that which can be done just as well now. The old proverb is full of truth and meaning, 'Whatever is worth doing at all, is worth doing well.' Many a man acquires a fortune by doing his business thoroughly, while his neighbor remains poor for life, because he only half does it. Ambition, energy, industry, perseverance, are indispensable requisites for success in business.

Fortune always favors the brave, and never helps a man who does not help himself. It won't do to spend your time like Mr Micawber, in waiting for something to 'turn up'. To such men one of two things usually 'turns up': the poorhouse or the jail; for idleness breeds bad habits, and clothes a man in rags. The poor spendthrift vagabond says to a rich man:

'I have discovered there is enough money in the world for all of us, if it was equally divided; this must be done, and we shall all be happy together.'

'But,' was the response, 'if everybody was like you, it would be spent in two months, and what would you do then?'

'Oh! divide again; keep dividing, of course!'

I was recently reading in a London paper an account of a like philosophic pauper who was kicked out of a cheap boarding-house because he could not pay his bill, but he had a roll of papers sticking out of his coat pocket, which, upon examination, proved to be his plan for paying off the national debt of England without the aid of a penny. People have got to do as [Oliver] Cromwell said: 'Not only trust in Providence, but keep the powder dry.' Do your part of the work, or you cannot succeed. Mahomet, one night, while encamping in the desert, overheard one of his fatigued followers remark: 'I will loose my camel, and trust it to God!' 'No, no, not so,' said the prophet, 'tie thy camel, and trust it to God!' Do all you can for yourselves, and then trust to Providence, or luck, or whatever you please to call it, for the rest.

Depend Upon Your Own Personal Exertions

The eye of the employer is often worth more than the hands of a dozen employees. In the nature of things, an agent cannot be so faithful to his employer as to himself. Many who are employers will call to mind instances where the best employees have overlooked important points which could not have escaped their own observation as a proprietor. No man has a right to expect to succeed in life unless he understands his business, and nobody can understand his business thoroughly unless he learns it by personal application and experience. A man may be a manufacturer: he has got to learn the many details of his business personally; he will learn something every day, and he will find he will make mistakes nearly every day. And these very mistakes are helps to him in the way of experiences if he but heeds them. He will be like the Yankee tin-peddler, who, having been cheated as to quality in the purchase of his merchandise, said: 'All right, there's a little information to be gained every day; I will never be cheated in that way again.' Thus a man buys his experience, and it is the best kind if not purchased at too dear a rate.

I hold that every man should, like Cuvier, the French naturalist, thoroughly know his business. So proficient was he in the study of natural history, that you might bring to him the bone, or even a section of a bone of an animal which he had never seen described, and, reasoning from analogy, he would be able to draw a picture of the object from which the bone had been taken. On one occasion his students attempted to deceive him. They rolled one of their number in a cow skin and put him under the professor's table as a new specimen. When the philosopher came into the room, some of the students asked him what animal it was. Suddenly the animal said, 'I am the devil and I am going to eat you.' It was but natural that Cuvier should desire to classify this creature, and examining it intently, he said:

'Divided hoof; graminivorous! It cannot be done.'

He knew that an animal with a split hoof must live upon grass and grain, or other kind of vegetation, and would not be inclined to eat flesh, dead or alive, so he considered himself perfectly safe. The possession of a perfect knowledge of your business is an absolute necessity in order to insure success.

Achievement

Among the maxims of the elder Rothschild was one, all apparent paradox: 'Be cautious and bold.' This seems to be a contradiction in terms, but it is not, and there is great wisdom in the maxim. It is, in fact, a condensed statement of what I have already said. It is to say; 'You must exercise your caution in laying your plans, but be bold in carrying them out.' A man who is all caution, will never dare to take hold and be successful; and a man who is all boldness is merely reckless, and must eventually fail. A man may go on to 'change' and make fifty, or one hundred thousand dollars in speculating in stocks, at a single operation. But if he has simple boldness without caution, it is mere chance, and what he gains to-day he will lose to-morrow. You must have both the caution and the boldness to insure success.

The Rothschilds have another maxim: 'Never have anything to do with an unlucky man or place.' That is to say, never have anything to do with a man or place which never succeeds, because, although a man may appear to be honest and intelligent, yet if he tries this or that thing and always fails, it is on account of some fault or infirmity that you may not be able to discover but nevertheless which must exist.

There is no such thing in the world as luck. There never was a man who could go out in the morning and find a purse full of gold in the street to-day, and another to-morrow, and so on, day after day: He may do so once in his life; but so far as mere luck is concerned, he is as liable to lose it as to find it. 'Like causes produce like effects.' If a man adopts the proper methods to be successful, 'luck' will not prevent him. If he does not succeed, there are reasons for it, although, perhaps, he may not be able to see them...

Don't Get Above Your Business

Young men after they get through their business training, or apprenticeship, instead of pursuing their avocation and rising in their business, will often lie about doing nothing. They say; 'I have learned my business, but I am not going to be a hireling; what is the object of learning my trade or profession, unless I establish myself?'

'Have you capital to start with?'

'No, but I am going to have it.'

'How are you going to get it?'

'I will tell you confidentially; I have a wealthy old aunt, and she will die pretty soon; but if she does not, I expect to find some rich old man who will lend me a few thousands to give me a start. If I only get the money to start with I will do well.'

Achievement

There is no greater mistake than when a young man believes he will succeed with borrowed money. Why? Because every man's experience coincides with that of Mr Astor, who said, 'It was more difficult for him to accumulate his first thousand dollars, than all the succeeding millions that made up his colossal fortune.' Money is good for nothing unless you know the value of it by experience. Give a boy twenty thousand dollars and put him in business, and the chances are that he will lose every dollar of it before he is a year older. Like buying a ticket in the lottery; and drawing a prize, it is 'easy come, easy go'. He does not know the value of it; nothing is worth anything, unless it costs effort. Without self-denial and economy; patience and perseverance, and commencing with capital which you have not earned, you are not sure to succeed in accumulating. Young men, instead of 'waiting for dead men's shoes', should be up and doing, for there is no class of persons who are so unaccommodating in regard to dying as these rich old people, and it is fortunate for the expectant heirs that it is so. Nine out of ten of the rich men of our country to-day, started out in life as poor boys, with determined wills, industry, perseverance, economy and good habits. They went on gradually, made their own money and saved it; and this is the best way to acquire a fortune. Stephen Girard started life as a poor cabin boy, and died worth nine million dollars. A.T. Stewart was a poor Irish boy; and he paid taxes on a million and a half dollars of income, per year. John Jacob Astor was a poor farmer boy, and died worth twenty millions. Cornelius Vanderbilt began life rowing a boat from Staten Island to New York; he presented our government with a steamship worth a million of dollars, and died worth fifty million. 'There is no royal road to learning,' says the proverb, and I may say it is equally true, 'there is no royal road to wealth.' But I think there is a royal road to both. The road to learning is a royal one; the road that enables the student to expand his intellect and add every day to his stock of knowledge, until, in the pleasant process of intellectual growth, he is able to solve the most profound problems, to count the stars, to analyze every atom of the globe, and to measure the firmament this is a regal highway, and it is the only road worth traveling...

Do Not Scatter Your Powers

Engage in one kind of business only, and stick to it faithfully until you succeed, or until your experience shows that you should abandon it. A constant hammering on one nail will generally drive it home at last, so that it can be clinched. When a man's undivided attention is centered on one object, his mind will constantly be suggesting improvements of value, which would escape him if his brain was occupied by a dozen different subjects at once. Many a fortune has slipped through a man's fingers because he was engaged in too many occupations at a time. There is good sense in the old caution against having too many irons in the fire at once.

Be Systematic

Men should be systematic in their business. A person who does business by rule, having a time and place for everything, doing his work promptly, will accomplish twice as much and with half the trouble of him who does it carelessly and slipshod. By introducing system into all your transactions, doing one thing at a time, always meeting appointments with punctuality, you find leisure for pastime and recreation; whereas the man who only half does one thing, and then turns to something else, and half does that, will have his business at loose ends, and will never know when his day's work is done, for it never will be done. Of course, there is a limit to all these rules. We must try to preserve the happy medium, for there is such a thing as being too systematic. There are men and women, for instance, who put away things so carefully that they can never find them again.

When the 'Astor House' was first started in New York city, it was undoubtedly the best hotel in the country. The proprietors had learned a good deal in Europe regarding hotels, and the landlords were proud of the rigid system which pervaded every department of their great establishment. When twelve o'clock at night had arrived, and there were a number of guests around, one of the proprietors would say, 'Touch that bell, John;' and in two minutes sixty servants, with a water-bucket in each hand, would present themselves in the hall. 'This,' said the landlord, addressing his guests, 'is our fire-bell; it will show you we are quite safe here; we do everything systematically.' This was before the Croton water was introduced into the city. But they sometimes carried their system too far. On one occasion, when the hotel was thronged with guests, one of the waiters was suddenly indisposed, and although there were fifty waiters in the hotel, the landlord thought he must have his full complement, or his 'system' would be interfered with. Just before dinner-time, he rushed down stairs and said, 'There must be another waiter, I am one waiter short, what can I do?' He happened to see 'Boots', the Irishman.

Achievement

'Pat,' said he, 'wash your hands and face; take that white apron and come into the dining-room in five minutes.' Presently Pat appeared as required, and the proprietor said: 'Now Pat, you must stand behind these two chairs, and wait on the gentlemen who will occupy them; did you ever act as a waiter?'

'I know all about it, sure, but I never did it.'

Like the Irish pilot, on one occasion when the captain, thinking he was considerably out of his course, asked, 'Are you certain you understand what you are doing?'

Pat replied, 'Sure and I knows every rock in the channel.'

That moment, 'bang' thumped the vessel against a rock.

'Ah! be-jabers, and that is one of 'em,' continued the pilot. But to return to the dining-room. 'Pat,' said the landlord, 'here we do everything systematically. You must first give the gentlemen each a plate of soup, and when they finish that, ask them what they will have next.'

Pat replied, 'Ah! an' I understand parfectly the vartues of shystem.'

Very soon in came the guests. The plates of soup were placed before them. One of Pat's two gentlemen ate his soup; the other did not care for it. He said:

'Waiter, take this plate away and bring me some fish.' Pat looked at the untasted plate of soup, and remembering the instructions of the landlord in regard to 'system,' replied: 'Not till ye have ate yer supe!'

Of course that was carrying 'system' entirely too far.

Strive for Perfection and You Will Reach Excellence

J.R.D. Tata

Jehangir Ratanji Dadabhoy Tata (1904–1993) was a French-born Indian aviator, entrepreneur and chairman of the Tata Group. He was the first licensed pilot in India and best known for founding several industries under the Tata Group, including Tata Consultancy Services, Tata Motors, Titan Industries, Tata Salt, Voltas and Air India. In the following extract from The Joy of Achievement: Conversations with J.R.D. Tata *(1995) by R.M. Lala, the tycoon shares the secret of his managerial success: listening to others, treating every individual according to their character—in order to draw the best out of them—and timely delegation to the experts.*

~

'*Despite all the difficulties, all the frustrations, there is a joy in having done something as well as you could and better than others thought you could.*'
 —J.R.D. Tata, on the fiftieth anniversary flight of his launching civil aviation in India

Achievement

The Art of Management

When asked about his approach to people management, J.R.D. said that he had made mistakes like everybody else. For instance, he said he had been criticized for being too much of a consensus man. He admitted that he did not like taking unilateral decisions.

J.R.D.: I am disinclined to take hard decisions because they would create unpleasantness. But I personally feel, though I may be wrong, that keeping a certain constancy in the way people regard you, in the way you relate to people, will result in a good net result over the long-term. You know, it is like a family. You can't make strong, hard decisions throughout, fire so and so, get rid of so and so, back up one side of the family rather than another. I know that all my colleagues have their own views, and on many views of theirs I don't agree and they don't agree perhaps with mine. But generally, we have always come to feel that we are doing the best we can and that we are sincere and that we mean to do the right thing.

Getting the Best Out of Others

J.R.D.: When a number of persons are involved I am definitely a consensus man. But that does not mean that I do not express my views. But basically, it is a question of having to deal with individual men heading different enterprises. And with each man I have my own way. I am one who will make full allowance for a man's character and idiosyncrasies. You have to adapt yourself to their ways and deal accordingly and draw out the best in each man... It may be that because all others were older than me when I became the chairman [at 34] I became a consensus man... If I have any merit, it is getting on with individuals according to their ways and characteristics. At times it involves suppressing yourself. It is painful but necessary... To be a leader you have got to lead human beings with affection.

J.R.D.'s Golden Rule for Success

J.R.D. had one rule that he said was essential for anything worthwhile to be achieved—'Strive for perfection and you will reach excellence.' I once asked him what the secret of his success in business was. He shook his head. 'No secret, just long hours. I used to put in seventy-five to eighty hours of work a week.' He then added rather mischievously, 'You know something? I do not like to work. I like to be interrupted.'

ACHIEVEMENT

Guiding Principles

When a teacher in Calcutta asked J.R.D. to list his 'guiding principles' he summarized them as follows:

- Nothing worthwhile is ever achieved without deep thought and hard work.
- One must think for oneself and never accept at face value slogans and catchphrases to which, unfortunately, our people are too easily susceptible.
- One must forever strive for excellence or even perfection in any task, however small, and never be satisfied with second best.
- No success or achievement in material terms is worthwhile unless it serves the needs or interests of the country and its people, and is achieved by fair and honest means.
- Good human relations not only bring great personal rewards but are essential to the success of any enterprise.

How J.R.D. Saw Himself

J.R.D.: I had no training in management but when I started in in 1926, some books on management were being written. Not having had an academic training in engineering and technology, my only contribution to management had to be in handling men who had been so trained. Every man has his own way of doing things. To get the best out of them is to let them exploit their own instincts and only intervene when you think they are going wrong. Therefore all my management contributions were on the human aspect through inducing, convincing and encouraging the human being. The exception was in the field of aviation, where I knew the technical side and perhaps half my love for aviation comes from the fact that it was the only field in which I have felt competent.

One thing I regret is never having been in line-management except in the airlines. In other fields decisions I took had to be executed by someone else. As I had no technical training, I always liked to consult the experts. At times I felt like a soldier who has never been an officer catapulted to be a General. When I have to make a decision I feel I must first make sure that the superior knowledge of my advisers confirms the soundness of my decision; secondly, that they would execute my decision not reluctantly but being convinced about it; thirdly, I see myself in Tatas as the leader of a team, who has to weigh the impact of any decision on other Tata companies, on the unity of the group. I think this policy has paid off.

Beat Stress and Adopt Good Working Habits

DALE CARNEGIE

Dale Carnegie (1888–1955) was an internationally renowned motivational speaker, writer and thinker. He was the author of How to Win Friends and Influence People *and* How to Stop Worrying and Start Living, *both of which are bestsellers even today. In the following piece, Carnegie illustrates how we can beat paralyzing stress by focusing on our day-to-day objectives. Worrying not only hampers our mental health and clarity but it also affects us physically. Stating the facts, analyzing our problems and acting on the solutions is the key to entrepreneurial progress.*

~

If you want to avoid worry, do what Sir William Osler did: Live in 'day-tight compartments'. Don't stew about the future. Just live each day until bedtime. And the next time Trouble—with a capital T—comes gunning for you and backs you up in a corner, try the magic formula of Willis H. Carrier. And always remind yourself of the exorbitant price you can pay for worry in terms of your health.

~

Achievement

In the spring of 1871, a young man picked up a book and read twenty-one words that had a profound effect on his future. A medical student at the Montreal General Hospital, he was worried about passing the final examination, worried about what to do, where to go, how to build up a practice, how to make a living.

The twenty-one words that this young medical student read in 1871 helped him to become the most famous physician of his generation. He organised the world-famous Johns Hopkins School of Medicine. He became Regius Professor of Medicine at Oxford—the highest honour that can be bestowed upon any medical man in the British Empire. He was knighted by the King of England. When he died, two huge volumes containing 1,466 pages were required to tell the story of his life.

His name was Sir William Osler. Here are the twenty-one words that he read in the spring of 1871— twenty-one words from Thomas Carlyle that helped him lead a life free from worry: 'Our main business is not to see what lies dimly at a distance, but to do what lies clearly at hand.'

Forty-two years later, on a soft spring night when the tulips were blooming on the campus, this man, Sir William Osler, addressed the students of Yale University. He told those Yale students that a man like himself who had been a professor in four universities and had written a popular book was supposed to have 'brains of a special quality'. He declared that that was untrue. He said that his intimate friends knew that his brains were 'of the most mediocre character.'

What, then, was the secret of his success? He stated that it was owing to what he called living in 'day-tight compartments'. What did he mean by that? A few months before he spoke at Yale, Sir William Osler had crossed the Atlantic on a great ocean liner where the captain standing on the bridge, could press a button and—presto!—there was a clanging of machinery and various parts of the ship were immediately shut off from one another—shut off into watertight compartments. 'Now each one of you,' Dr Osler said to those Yale students, 'is a much more marvelous organisation than the great liner, and bound on a longer voyage. What I urge is that you so learn to control the machinery as to live with "day-tight compartments" as the most certain way to ensure safety on the voyage. Get on the bridge, and see that at least the great bulkheads are in working order. Touch a button and hear, at every level of your life, the iron doors shutting out the Past—the dead yesterdays. Touch another and shut off, with a metal curtain, the Future—the unborn tomorrows. Then you are safe—safe for today! Shut off the past!

ACHIEVEMENT

Let the dead past bury its dead. Shut out the yesterdays which have lighted fools the way to dusty death. The load of tomorrow, added to that of yesterday, carried today, makes the strongest falter. Shut off the future as tightly as the past. The future is today.

There is no tomorrow. The day of man's salvation is now. Waste of energy, mental distress, nervous worries dog the steps of a man who is anxious about the future. Shut close, then the great fore and aft bulkheads, and prepare to cultivate the habit of life of "day-tight compartments".

Did Dr Osler mean to say that we should not make any effort to prepare for tomorrow? No. Not at all. But he did go on in that address to say that the best possible way to prepare for tomorrow is to concentrate with all your intelligence, all your enthusiasm, on doing today's work superbly today. That is the only possible way you can prepare for the future.

~

Would you like a quick, sure-fire recipe for handling worry situations—a technique you can start using right away? Then let me tell you about the method worked out by Willis H. Carrier, the brilliant engineer who launched the air-conditioning industry…

'When I was a young man,' Mr Carrier said, 'I

worked for the Buffalo Forge Company in Buffalo, New York. I was handed the assignment of installing a gas-cleaning device in a plant of the Pittsburgh Plate Glass Company at Crystal City, Missouri—a plant costing millions of dollars. The purpose of this installation was to remove the impurities from the gas so it could be burned without injuring the engines. This method of cleaning gas was new. It had been tried only once before—and under different conditions. In my work at Crystal City, Missouri, unforeseen difficulties arose. It worked after a fashion—but not well enough to meet the guarantee we had made.

'I was stunned by my failure. It was almost as if someone had struck me a blow on the head. My stomach, my insides, began to twist and turn. For a while I was so worried I couldn't sleep.

'Finally, common sense reminded me that worry wasn't getting me anywhere; so I figured out a way to handle my problem without worrying. It worked superbly. I have been using this same anti-worry technique for more than thirty years. It is simple. Anyone can use it. It consists of three steps:

'*Step I.* I analysed the situation fearlessly and honestly and figured out what was the worst that could possibly happen as a result of this failure.

No one was going to jail me or shoot me. That was certain. True, there was a chance that I would lose my position; and there was also a chance that my employers would have to remove the machinery and lose the twenty thousand dollars we had invested.

'*Step II.* After figuring out what was the worst that could possibly happen, I reconciled myself to accepting it, if necessary. I said to myself: This failure will be a blow to my record, and it might possibly mean the loss of my job; but if it does, I can always get another position. Conditions could be much worse; and as far as my employers are concerned—well, they realize that we are experimenting with a new method of cleaning gas, and if this experience costs them twenty thousand dollars, they can stand it. They can charge it up to research, for it is an experiment.

'After discovering the worst that could possibly happen and reconciling myself to accepting it, if necessary, an extremely important thing happened: I immediately relaxed and felt a sense of peace that I hadn't experienced in days.

'*Step III.* From that time on, I calmly devoted my time and energy to trying to improve upon the worst which I had already accepted mentally.

'I now tried to figure out ways and means by which I might reduce the loss of twenty thousand dollars that we faced. I made several tests and finally figured out that if we spent another five thousand for additional equipment, our problem would be solved. We did this, and instead of the firm losing twenty thousand, we made fifteen thousand.

'I probably would never have been able to do this if I had kept on worrying, because one of the worst features about worrying is that it destroys our ability to concentrate. When we worry, our minds jump here and there and everywhere, and we lose all power of decision. However, when we force ourselves to face the worst and accept it mentally, we then eliminate all those vague imaginings and put ourselves in a position in which we are able to concentrate on our problem.

'This incident that I have related occurred many years ago. It worked so superbly that I have been using it ever since; and, as a result, my life has been almost completely free from worry.'

Now, why is Willis H. Carrier's magic formula so valuable and so practical, psychologically speaking? Because it yanks us down out of the great grey clouds in which we fumble around when we are blinded by worry. It plants our feet good and solid on the earth. We know where we stand. And if we haven't solid ground under us, how in creation can we ever hope to think anything through?

~

Would you like to see how someone else adopted Willis H. Carrier's magic formula and applied it to his own problem? Well, here is one example, from a New York oil dealer who was a student in my classes.

'I was being blackmailed!' this student began. 'I didn't believe it was possible—I didn't believe it could happen outside of the movies—but I was actually being blackmailed! What happened was this: the oil company of which I was the head had a number of delivery trucks and a number of drivers. At that time, OPA regulations were strictly in force, and we were rationed on the amount of oil we could deliver to any one of our customers. I didn't know it, but it seems that certain of our drivers had been delivering oil short to our regular customers, and then reselling the surplus to customers of their own.

'The first inkling I had of these illegitimate transactions was when a man who claimed to be a government inspector came to see me one day and demanded hush money. He had got documentary proof of what our drivers had been doing, and he threatened to turn this proof over to the District Attorney's office if I didn't cough up.

'I knew, of course, that I had nothing to worry about—personally, at least. But I also knew that the law says a firm is responsible for the actions of its employees. What's more, I knew that if the case came to court, and it was aired in the newspapers, the bad publicity would ruin my business. And I was proud of my business—it had been founded by my father twenty-four years before.

'I was so worried I was sick! I didn't eat or sleep for three days and nights. I kept going around in crazy circles. Should I pay the money—five thousand dollars—or should I tell this man to go ahead and do his damnedest? Either way I tried to make up my mind, it ended in nightmare.

'Then, on Sunday night, I happened to pick up the booklet on *How to Stop Worrying* which I had been given in my Carnegie class in public speaking. I started to read it, and came across the story of Willis H. Carrier. "Face the worst," it said. So I asked myself: "What is the worst that can happen if I refuse to pay up, and these blackmailers turn their records over to the District Attorney?"

'The answer to that was: The ruin of my business—that's the worst that can happen. I can't go to jail. All that can happen is that I shall be ruined by the publicity.

ACHIEVEMENT

'I then said to myself: "All right, the business is ruined. I accept that mentally. What happens next?"

'Well, with my business ruined, I would probably have to look for a job. That wasn't bad. I knew a lot about oil—there were several firms that might be glad to employ me. I began to feel better. The blue funk I had been in for three days and nights began to lift a little. My emotions calmed down. And to my astonishment, I was able to think.

'I was clear-headed enough now to face Step III—improve on the worst. As I thought of solutions, an entirely new angle presented itself to me. If I told my attorney the whole situation, he might find a way out which I hadn't thought of. I know it sounds stupid to say that this hadn't even occurred to me before—but of course I hadn't been thinking, I had only been worrying! I immediately made up my mind that I would see my attorney first thing in the morning—and then I went to bed and slept like a log!

'How did it end? Well, the next morning my lawyer told me to go and see the District Attorney and tell him the truth. I did precisely that. When I finished I was astonished to hear the D.A. say that this blackmail racket had been going on for months and that the man who claimed to be a "government agent" was a crook wanted by the police. What a relief to hear all this after I had tormented myself for three days and nights wondering whether I should hand over five thousand dollars to this professional swindler!

'This experience taught me a lasting lesson. Now, whenever I face a pressing problem that threatens to worry me, I give it what I call "the old Willis H. Carrier formula".'

~

The great Nobel-Prize winner in medicine, Dr Alexis Carrel, said: 'Business men who do not know how to fight worry die young.' And so do housewives and horse doctors and bricklayers.

A few years ago, I spent my vacation motoring through Texas and New Mexico with Dr O.F. Gober—one of the medical executives of the Santa Fe railway. His exact title was chief physician of the Gulf, Colorado and Santa Fe Hospital Association. We got to talking about the effects of worry, and he said: 'Seventy per cent of all patients who come to physicians could cure themselves if they only got rid of their fears and worries. Don't think for a moment that I mean that their ills are imaginary,' he said. 'Their ills are as real as a throbbing toothache and sometimes a hundred times more serious. I refer to such illnesses as nervous indigestion, some stomach ulcers, heart disturbances, insomnia, some headaches, and some types of paralysis.

'These illnesses are real. I know what I am talking about,' said Dr Gober, 'for I myself suffered from a stomach ulcer for twelve years.

'Fear causes worry. Worry makes you tense and nervous and affects the nerves of your stomach and actually changes the gastric juices of your stomach from normal to abnormal and often leads to stomach ulcers.'

Dr Joseph F. Montague, author of the book *Nervous Stomach Trouble*, says much the same thing. He says: 'You do not get stomach ulcers from what you eat. You get ulcers from what is eating you.'

Dr W.C. Alvarez, of the Mayo Clinic, said, 'Ulcers frequently flare up or subside according to the hills and valleys of emotional stress.'

That statement was backed up by a study of 15,000 patients treated for stomach disorders at the Mayo Clinic. Four out of five had no physical basis whatever for their stomach illnesses. Fear, worry, hate, supreme selfishness, and the inability to adjust themselves to the world of reality—these were largely the causes of their stomach illnesses and stomach ulcers. Stomach ulcers can kill you…

Can any man possibly be a success who is paying

for business advancement with stomach ulcers and heart trouble? What shall it profit a man if he gains the whole world—and loses his health? Even if he owned the whole world, he could sleep in only one bed at a time and eat only three meals a day...

Do you love life? Do you want to live long and enjoy good health? Here is how you can do it. I am quoting Dr Alexis Carrel again. He said: 'Those who keep the peace of their inner selves in the midst of the tumult of the modern city are immune from nervous diseases.'

Can you keep the peace of your inner self in the midst of the tumult of a modern city? If you are a normal person, the answer is 'yes'. 'Emphatically yes.' Most of us are stronger than we realise. We have inner resources that we have probably never tapped. As Thoreau said in his immortal book, *Walden*:

> I know of no more encouraging fact than the unquestionable ability of man to elevate his life by a conscious endeavour. If one advances confidently in the direction of his dreams, and endeavours to live the life he has imagined, he will meet with a success unexpected in common hours.

Surely, many of the readers of this book have as much will power and as many inner resources as Olga K. Jarvey has...

Achievement

Here is Olga K. Jarvey's story as she wrote it for me: 'Eight and a half years ago, I was condemned to die—a slow, agonising death—of cancer. The best medical brains of the country, the Mayo brothers, confirmed the sentence. I was at a dead-end street, the ultimate gaped at me! I was young. I did not want to die! In my desperation, I phoned my doctor at Kellogg and cried out to him the despair in my heart. Rather impatiently he upbraided me: "What's the matter, Olga, haven't you any fight in you? Sure, you will die if you keep on crying. Yes, the worst has overtaken you. O.K.—face the facts! Quit worrying! And then do something about it!" Right then and there I took an oath, an oath so solemn that the nails sank deep into my flesh and cold chills ran down my spine: "I am not going to worry! I am not going to cry! And if there is anything to mind over matter, I am going to win! I am going to LIVE!"

'The usual amount of X-ray in such advanced cases, where they cannot apply radium, is 10 1/2 minutes a day for 30 days. They gave me X-ray for 14 1/2 minutes a day for 49 days; and although my bones stuck out of my emaciated body like rocks on a barren hillside, and although my feet were like lead, I did not worry! Not once did I cry! I smiled! Yes, I actually forced myself to smile.

'I am not so foolish as to imagine that merely smiling can cure cancer. But I do believe that a cheerful mental attitude helps the body fight disease. At any rate, I experienced one of the miracle cures of cancer. I have never been healthier than in the last few years, thanks to those challenging, fighting words of Dr McCaffery: "Face the facts: Quit worrying; then do something about it!"'

The Essential Techniques of Problem Analysis

We must equip ourselves to deal with different kinds of worries by learning the three basic steps of problem analysis. The three steps are: 1. Get the facts. 2. Analyse the facts. 3. Arrive at a decision—and then act on that decision. Obvious stuff? Yes, Aristotle taught it—and used it. And you and I must use it too if we are going to solve the problems that are harassing us and turning our days and nights into veritable hells.

Let me show you all this as it works out in practice. Since the Chinese say one picture is worth ten thousand words, suppose I show you a picture of how one man put exactly what we are talking about into concrete action.

Let's take the case of Galen Litchfield—a man I have known for several years; one of the most successful American business men in the Far East.

Achievement

Mr Litchfield was in China in 1942, when the Japanese invaded Shanghai. And here is his story as he told it to me while a guest in my home:

'Shortly after the Japs took Pearl Harbour,' Galen Litchfield began, 'they came swarming into Shanghai. I was the manager of the Asia Life Insurance Company in Shanghai. They sent us an "army liquidator"—he was really an admiral—and gave me orders to assist this man in liquidating our assets. I didn't have any choice in the matter. I could co-operate—or else. And the "or else" was certain death.

'I went through the motions of doing what I was told, because I had no alternative. But there was one block of securities, worth $750,000, which I left off the list I gave to the admiral. I left that block of securities off the list because they belonged to our Hong Kong organisation and had nothing to do with the Shanghai assets. All the same, I feared I might be in hot water if the Japs found out what I had done. And they soon found out.

'I wasn't in the office when the discovery was made, but my head accountant was there. He told me that the Jap admiral flew into a rage, and stamped and swore, and called me a thief and a traitor! I had defied the Japanese Army! I knew what that meant. I would be thrown into the Bridge house!

'The Bridge house! The torture chamber of the Japanese Gestapo! I had had personal friends who had killed themselves rather than be taken to that prison. I had had other friends who had died in that place after ten days of questioning and torture. Now I was slated for the Bridge house myself!

'What did I do? I heard the news on Sunday afternoon. I suppose I should have been terrified. And I would have been terrified if I hadn't had a definite technique for solving my problems. For years, whenever I was worried I had always gone to my typewriter and written down two questions—and the answers to these questions:

1. What am I worrying about?
2. What can I do about it?

'I used to try to answer those questions without writing them down. But I stopped that years ago. I found that writing down both the questions and the answers clarifies my thinking. So, that Sunday afternoon, I went directly to my room at the Shanghai Y.M.C.A. and got out my typewriter. I wrote:

1. What am I worrying about?

I am afraid I will be thrown into the Bridge house tomorrow morning.

'Then I typed out the second question:

2. What can I do about it?

ACHIEVEMENT

'I spent hours thinking out and writing down the four courses of action I could take—and what the probable consequence of each action would be.

1. I can try to explain to the Japanese admiral. But he 'no speak English'. If I try to explain to him through an interpreter, I may stir him up again. That might mean death, for he is cruel, would rather dump me in the Bridge house than bother talking about it.

2. I can try to escape. Impossible. They keep track of me all the time. I have to check in and out of my room at the Y.M.C.A. If I try to escape, I'll probably be captured and shot.

3. I can stay here in my room and not go near the office again. If I do, the Japanese admiral will be suspicious, will probably send soldiers to get me and throw me into the Bridgehouse without giving me a chance to say a word.

4. I can go down to the office as usual on Monday morning. If I do, there is a chance that the Japanese admiral may be so busy that he will not think of what I did. Even if he does think of it, he may have cooled off and may not bother me. If this happens, I am all right. Even if he does bother me, I'll still have a chance to try to explain to him. So, going down to the office as usual on Monday morning, and acting as if nothing had gone wrong gives me two chances to escape the Bridgehouse.

'As soon as I thought it all out and decided to accept the fourth plan—to go down to the office as usual on Monday morning—I felt immensely relieved.

'When I entered the office the next morning, the Japanese admiral sat there with a cigarette dangling from his mouth. He glared at me as he always did; and said nothing. Six weeks later—thank God—he went back to Tokyo and my worries were ended.

'As I have already said, I probably saved my life by sitting down that Sunday afternoon and writing out all the various steps I could take and then writing down the probable consequences of each step and calmly coming to a decision. If I hadn't done that, I might have floundered and hesitated and done the wrong thing on the spur of the moment. If I hadn't thought out my problem and come to a decision, I would have been frantic with worry all Sunday afternoon. I wouldn't have slept that night. I would have gone down to the office Monday morning with a harassed and worried look; and that alone might have aroused the suspicion of the Japanese admiral and spurred him to act.

'Experience has proved to me, time after time, the enormous value of arriving at a decision. It is the failure to arrive at a fixed purpose, the inability to stop going round and round in maddening circles, that drives men to nervous breakdowns and living hells. I find that fifty per cent of my worries vanishes once I arrive at a clear, definite decision; and another forty per cent usually vanishes once I start to carry out that decision.

'So I banish about ninety per cent of my worries by taking these four steps:

1. Writing down precisely what I am worrying about.

2. Writing down what I can do about it.

3. Deciding what to do.

4. Starting immediately to carry out that decision.'

Why is [Galen Litchfield's] method so superb? Because it is efficient, concrete, and goes directly to the heart of the problem. On top of all that, it is climaxed by the third and indispensable rule: Do something about it. Unless we carry out our action, all our fact-finding and analysis is whistling upwind—it's a sheer waste of energy.

Why don't you employ Galen Litchfield's technique to one of your worries right now?

Question No. 1: What am I worrying about?

Question No. 2: What can I do about it?

Question No. 3: Here is what I am going to do about it.

Question No. 4: When am I going to start doing it?

Solving Worry Problems at Work

Now I am going to show you how one business executive eliminated not fifty per cent of his worries, but seventy-five per cent of all the time he formerly spent in conferences, trying to solve business problems... This concerns a very real person—Leon Shimkin, a partner and general manager of one of the foremost publishing houses in the United States: Simon and Schuster.

Here is Leon Shimkin's experience in his own words:

'For fifteen years I spent almost half of every business day holding conferences, discussing problems. Should we do this or that—do nothing at all? We would get tense; twist in our chairs; walk the floor; argue and go around in circles. When night came, I would be utterly exhausted. I fully expected to go on doing this sort of thing for the rest of my life. I had been doing it for fifteen years, and it never occurred to me that there was a better way of doing it. If anyone had told me that I could eliminate three-fourths of all the time I spent in those worried conferences, and three-fourths of my nervous strain—I would have thought he was a wild-eyed, slap-happy, armchair optimist. Yet I devised a plan that did just that. I have been using this plan for eight years. It has performed wonders for my efficiency, my health, and my happiness.

'It sounds like magic—but like all magic tricks, it is extremely simple when you see how it is done.

'Here is the secret: First, I immediately stopped the procedure I had been using in my conferences for fifteen years—a procedure that began with my troubled associates reciting all the details of what had gone wrong, and ending up by asking: "What shall we do?" Second, I made a new rule—a rule that everyone who wishes to present a problem to me must first prepare and submit a memorandum answering these four questions:

Question 1: What is the problem?

('In the old days we used to spend an hour or two in a worried conference without anyone's knowing specifically and concretely what the real problem was. We used to work ourselves into a lather discussing our troubles without ever troubling to write out specifically what our problem was.)

Question 2: What is the cause of the problem?

('As I look back over my career, I am appalled at the wasted hours I have spent in worried conferences without ever trying to find out clearly the conditions which lay at the root of the problem.)

Question 3: What are all possible solutions of the problem?

('In the old days, one man in the conference would suggest one solution. Someone else would argue with him. Tempers would flare. We would often get clear off the subject, and at the end of the conference no one would have written down all the various things we could do to attack the problem.)

Question 4: What solution do you suggest?

('I used to go into a conference with a man who had spent hours worrying about a situation and going around in circles without ever once thinking through all possible solutions and then writing down: "This is the solution I recommend."')

'My associates rarely come to me now with their problems. Why? Because they have discovered that in order to answer these four questions they have to get all the facts and think their problems through. And after they have done that they find, in three-fourths of the cases, they don't have to consult me at all, because the proper solution has popped out like a piece of bread popping out from an electric toaster. Even in those cases where consultation is necessary, the discussion takes about one-third the time formerly required, because it proceeds along an orderly, logical path to a reasoned conclusion.

'Much less time is now consumed in the house of Simon and Schuster in worrying and talking about what is wrong; and a lot more action is obtained toward making those things right.'

~

Another instance:

My friend, Frank Bettger, one of the top insurance men in America, tells me he not only reduced his business worries, but nearly doubled his income, by a similar method.

'Years ago,' says Frank Bettger, 'when I first started to sell insurance, I was filled with a boundless enthusiasm and love for my work. Then something happened. I became so discouraged that I despised my work and thought of giving it up. I think I would have quit—if I hadn't got the idea, one Saturday morning, of sitting down and trying to get at the root of my worries.

'1. I asked myself first: "Just what is the problem?" The problem was: that I was not getting high enough returns for the staggering amount of calls I was making. I seemed to do pretty well at selling a prospect, until the moment came for closing a sale. Then the customer would say: "Well, I'll think it over, Mr Bettger. Come and see me again." It was the time I wasted on these follow-up calls that was causing my depression.

'2. I asked myself: "What are the possible solutions?" But to get the answer to that one, I had to study the facts. I got out my record book for the last twelve months and studied the figures.

'I made an astounding discovery! Right there in black and white, I discovered that seventy per cent of my sales had been closed on the very first interview! Twenty-three per cent of my sales had been closed on the second interview! And only seven per cent of my sales had been closed on those third, fourth, fifth, etc., interviews, which were running me ragged and taking up my time. In other words, I was wasting fully one half of my working day on a part of my business which was responsible for only seven per cent of my sales!

'3. "What is the answer?" The answer was obvious. I immediately cut out all visits beyond the second interview, and spent the extra time building up new prospects. The results were unbelievable. In a very short time, I had almost doubled the cash value of every visit I made from a call!'

Can you apply these questions to your business problems? To repeat my challenge—they can reduce your worries by fifty per cent. Here they are again:

1. What is the problem?
2. What is the cause of the problem?

3. What are all possible solutions to the problem?
4. What solution do you suggest?

~

Adopt these Four Good Working Habits that will help prevent fatigue and worry:

Good working habit no. 1: Clear your desk of all papers except those relating to the immediate problem at hand.

Roland L. Williams, President of Chicago and North-western Railway, says: 'A person with his desk piled high with papers on various matters will find his work much easier and more accurate if he clears that desk of all but the immediate problem on hand. I call this good housekeeping, and it is the number-one step towards efficiency.'

If you visit the Library of Congress in Washington, D.C., you will find five words painted on the ceiling—five words written by the poet Pope: 'Order is Heaven's first law.'

Order ought to be the first law of business, too. But is it? No, the average business man's desk is cluttered up with papers that he hasn't looked at for weeks. In fact, the publisher of a New Orleans newspaper once told me that his secretary cleared up one of his desks and found a typewriter that had been missing for two years!

The mere sight of a desk littered with unanswered mail and reports and memos is enough to breed confusion, tension, and worries. It is much worse than that. The constant reminder of 'a million things to do and no time to do them' can worry you not only into tension and fatigue, but it can also worry you into high blood pressure, heart trouble, and stomach ulcers.

Dr John H. Stokes, professor, Graduate School of Medicine, University of Pennsylvania, read a paper before the National Convention of the American Medical Association—a paper entitled 'Functional Neuroses as Complications of Organic Disease'. In that paper, Dr Stokes listed eleven conditions under the title: 'What to Look for in the Patient's State of Mind'. Here is the first item on that list: 'The sense of must or obligation; the unending stretch of things ahead that simply have to be done.'

But how can such an elementary procedure as clearing your desk and making decisions help you avoid this high pressure, this sense of must, this sense of an 'unending stretch of things ahead that simply have to be done'? Dr William L. Sadler, the famous psychiatrist, tells of a patient who, by using this simple device, avoided a nervous breakdown. The man was an executive in a big Chicago firm. When he came to Dr Sadler's office, he was tense, nervous, worried. He knew he was heading for a tailspin, but he couldn't quit work. He had to have help.

'While this man was telling me his story,' Dr Sadler says, 'my telephone rang. It was the hospital calling; and, instead of deferring the matter, I took time right then to come to a decision. I always settle questions, if possible, right on the spot. I had no sooner hung up than the phone rang again. Again an urgent matter, which I took time to discuss. The third interruption came when a colleague of mine came to my office for advice on a patient who was critically ill. When I had finished with him, I turned to my caller and began to apologise for keeping him waiting. But he had brightened up. He had a completely different look on his face.'

'Don't apologise, doctor!' this man said to Sadler. 'In the last ten minutes, I think I've got a hunch as to what is wrong with me. I'm going back to my offices and revise my working habits. But before I go, do you mind if I take a look in your desk?'

Dr Sadler opened up the drawers of his desk. All empty—except for supplies. 'Tell me,' said the patient, 'where do you keep your unfinished business?'

'Finished!' said Sadler.

'And where do you keep your unanswered mail?'

'Answered!' Sadler told him. 'My rule is never to

lay down a letter until I have answered it. I dictate the reply to my secretary at once.'

Six weeks later, this same executive invited Dr Sadler to come to his office. He was changed—and so was his desk. He opened the desk drawers to show there was no unfinished business inside of the desk. 'Six weeks ago,' this executive said, 'I had three different desks in two different offices—and was snowed under by my work. I was never finished. After talking to you, I came back here and cleared out a wagon-load of reports and old papers. Now I work at one desk, settle things as they come up, and don't have a mountain of unfinished business nagging at me and making me tense and worried. But the most astonishing thing is I've recovered completely. There is nothing wrong any more with my health!'

Charles Evans Hughes, former Chief Justice of the United States Supreme Court, said: 'Men do not die from overwork. They die from dissipation and worry.' Yes, from dissipation of their energies—and worry because they never seem to get their work done.

Good working habit no. 2: Do things in the order of their importance.

Henry L. Dougherty, founder of the nation-wide Cities Service Company, said that regardless of how much salary he paid, there were two abilities he found it almost impossible to find.

Achievement

Those two priceless abilities are: first, the ability to think. Second, the ability to do things in the order of their importance.

Charles Luckman, the lad who started from scratch and climbed in twelve years to president of the Pepsodent Company, got a salary of a hundred thousand dollars a year, and made a million dollars besides—that lad declares that he owes much of his success to developing the two abilities that Henry L. Dougherty said he found almost impossible to find. Charles Luckman said: 'As far back as I can remember, I have got up at five o'clock in the morning because I can think better then than any other time—I can think better then and plan my day, plan to do things in the order of their importance.'

Franklin Bettger, one of America's most successful insurance salesmen, doesn't wait until five o'clock in the morning to plan his day. He plans it the night before—sets a goal for himself—a goal to sell a certain amount of insurance that day. If he fails, that amount is added to the next day—and so on.

I know from long experience that one is not always able to do things in the order of their importance, but I also know that some kind of plan to do first things first is infinitely better than extemporising as you go along.

If George Bernard Shaw had not made it a rigid rule to do first things first, he would probably have failed as a writer and might have remained a bank cashier all his life. His plan called for writing five pages each day. That plan and his dogged determination to carry it through saved him. That plan inspired him to go right on writing five pages a day for nine heartbreaking years, even though he made a total of only thirty dollars in those nine years—about a penny a day.

Good working habit no. 3: When you face a problem, solve it then and there if you have the facts necessary to make a decision. Don't keep putting off decisions.

One of my former students, the late H.P. Howell, told me that when he was a member of the board of directors of U.S. Steel, the meetings of the board were often long-drawn-out affairs—many problems were discussed, few decisions were made. The result: each member of the board had to carry home bundles of reports to study.

Finally, Mr Howell persuaded the board of directors to take up one problem at a time and come to a decision. No procrastination—no putting off. The decision might be to ask for additional facts; it might be to do something or do nothing. But a decision was reached on each problem before passing on to the next.

Mr Howell told me that the results were striking and salutary: the docket was cleared. The calendar was clean. No longer was it necessary for each member to carry home a bundle of reports. No longer was there a worried sense of unresolved problems.

A good rule, not only for the board of directors of U.S. Steel, but for you and me.

Good working habit no. 4: Learn to organise, deputise, and supervise.

Many a businessman is driving himself to a premature grave because he has never learned to delegate responsibility to others, insists on doing everything himself. Result: details and confusion overwhelm him. He is driven by a sense of hurry, worry, anxiety, and tension. It is hard to learn to delegate responsibilities. I know. It was hard for me, awfully hard. I also know from experience the disasters that can be caused by delegating authority to the wrong people. But difficult as it is to delegate authority, the executive must do it if he is to avoid worry, tension, and fatigue.

The Perseverence of Ardeshir Godrej

B.K. KARANJIA

Ardeshir Godrej (1868–1936) was not only the co-founder of the Godrej Group, but a pioneering inventor, businessman and a thorough patriot. At a time when the British ruled India and nobody trusted Indian products, he revolutionized Indian business through his sheer determination, attention to detail and ingenuity. He invented the springless lock—more secure than any other lock at the time—unbreakable, fire-resistant safes, soaps made out of vegetable oils, and filed countless other patents. Godrej brought respectability to Indian industry, aggressively marketing his products as 'Made in India', believing that self-reliance was the way to earn freedom. As the following excerpts from his biography Vijitatma: Pioneer-Founder Ardeshir Godrej *(2004) show, Ardeshir was a steadfast, principled man who was honest in his dealings, meticulous in his research and dogged in his pursuit of providing the best for his countrymen—all hallmarks of a great entrepreneur and leader.*

~

Achievement

After giving up his job as a lawyer in Zanzibar when he found out that he might have to lie for a client, Ardeshir gave up law and returned to Bombay. Despite failing to strike a deal to sell top quality 'Made in India' surgical instruments, he found another calling.

~

The Power of Self-Respect and Self-Belief

[Ardeshir] had got a job as assistant to a chemist. But this was only a means to an end. His aim was to manufacture goods that would beat the British ones in quality. He believed that only through self-reliance could the country become self-respecting and win freedom. In fact, that was the reason for coming to see Uncle. To start manufacture he needed a loan.

'Of course, I'll give you the loan.' But Merwanji [his father's friend and a respected businessman] couldn't resist laughing, teasing him: 'But surely your father would loan you what you want?'

'Of course, he would. But it wouldn't be the same thing,' Ardeshir replied. 'He would gift the amount to me. What I am asking for is not a gift but a loan which, be sure, I'll return.'

Merwanji smiled. Surely, Ardeshir was one of a kind. 'How much do you need?'

'Three thousand rupees.'

'And may I ask what you are going to manufacture?'

'Surgical instruments, to begin with.'

'But who's going to buy surgical instruments? Is there a demand for surgical instruments?' Merwanji expressed his surprise. 'All that are needed are being imported, I suppose.'

Ardeshir wasn't worried about that. 'What I'm trying to prove, Uncle, is that even such highly sophisticated instruments can be made by Indians in India. I'm making a point. I've come to you to help me make this point. Once it's made, and our reputation established, we will go on to manufacture items in greater popular demand.'

…A few minutes later Merwanji came down with a bundle of rupee notes…

Before Ardeshir could get up to thank him, Merwanji raised a hand and made him sit down again…

'I'd like to ask you something. You're young and inexperienced and I've known you since the time you learned to walk. As an old man I tend to worry. Are you sure this is the right decision you're taking—I mean making surgical instruments?'

'Uncle… The chemists with whom I'm working have assured me that if these instruments are up to their specifications, they'll undertake marketing

ACHIEVEMENT

them themselves, they'll even get some surgeons from J.J. Hospital to endorse them, they'll spend on advertising…

~

It was for the first time in several months that Ardeshir could enjoy a good night's sleep. All these past days, after a hard day's work, there was harder work still, sharpening, shaping, fashioning scalpels, forceps, pincers, scissors and the basic implements of the surgeon's trade, working till well past midnight. He was successful in obtaining the desired accuracy in all these instruments except for the hypodermic syringe (called 'Cleopatra's needle' for some reason he couldn't fathom), where he couldn't quite obtain the sharpness required for the hollow end. But he was confident that with time he could achieve this also.

The chemists he worked for had placed all the facilities required at his disposal, the raw material and the implements, and given their utmost cooperation, and they were more than satisfied with the first results. There was now the consideration of pricing and marketing them. A conference had been called this morning at which the shop's British proprietor was to be present. When recounting this to me, Ardeshir's nephew Sohrab couldn't recall the proprietor's name. It began with an 'R' he said, but whether it was Richard or Robert, he couldn't be sure. Also, he didn't want the chemist company's name to be mentioned. They had long since left India and he saw no point in reviving old recriminations.

~

Ardeshir… had a strange sense of fulfillment that a task considered impossible had been completed by him. He was further encouraged when the British proprietor who appeared to be of a genial temperament profusely congratulated him on his accomplishment. He wasn't interested in the discussion that followed regarding pricing, listing the city's major hospitals and other possible markets, adding to the existing staff of salesmen, acquainting them with the selling points of this new product. His sole interest was in advertising them as 'Made in India'. All through the discussion he had an uneasy feeling that this, which to him was the crux of the matter, wasn't being alluded to at all. When he raised it they looked at him as if he were out of his mind.

'Look, young man,' the proprietor rebuked him, 'you may be a first-class machinist, but we are discussing marketing here. Please don't misunderstand.

ACHIEVEMENT

I have high regard for your country. Now had this been, say, an Indian antique I'd have said by all means blazon it in bold type as "Made in India". But surgical instruments, no way!'

Ardeshir had a sinking feeling in his stomach. His voice shook uncontrollably as he said, 'Please try and understand. The whole purpose of my working long hours was to prove that India can manufacture surgical instruments, that we have the ability—'

'Your ability has never been doubted, but we are talking marketing strategy here. Two difficulties face us. Surgical instruments by their very nature have a limited demand, confined mainly to hospitals and surgeries. Then again, surgeons themselves are used to imported instruments. They'd be nervous about switching over to locally made ones in a matter of life and death.'

'But,' Ardeshir argued, 'your salesmen could convince them that these are as good as imported ones. They could persuade surgeons to at least give these a trial to convince themselves.'

'Young man, salesmen are not miracle workers. They cannot change mindsets. Had this been a new brand of coffee they'd have asked customers to taste it and find out for themselves. But surgical instruments are a dicey business. I'm prepared to wager—your own people wouldn't have faith in Indian surgical instruments.'

Ardeshir felt his anger rising. He tried to control his hands' trembling. 'That's because you have conditioned them to use British goods. You have driven Indian goods out of the market. You are killing our industries slowly and ruthlessly. On no account will I allow you to do the same with my product, made with my talent and my skills.'

'That's no way to talk.' The proprietor stood up. 'Please get this straight. Our company will not throw away money on marketing a product which the public are yet not conditioned to accept.'

'Then please get this straight too. I'm not going to allow you to market my product unless it is advertised as "Made in India". That's final.'

'Have it your way. We can't force you and we don't intend to. But you know, I feel sorry for you. You have undoubted talent and here's an opportunity I'm giving you to use it to make a lot of money. You're throwing the opportunity away.'

'You're right. But I think we Indians are just beginning to realise that self-respect is more important than money.'

'You know, Mr Godrej, British products are top sellers. We British are today on top of the world.'

'Well, I'm glad to hear that,' Ardeshir retorted. 'Because as you know, the world goes round and what's up has to come down.'

~

Ardeshir went to his corner of the shop and sat down. The two Indian salesmen present at the meeting came down to commiserate with him and express their admiration for the stand he had taken. He kept quiet. Why hadn't they taken this stand at the meeting? They were Indians too, but he couldn't really blame them. The slavish mentality was all too prevalent. Only self-reliance could bring about self-respect, and it would take a long long time. Suddenly he felt sad and weary… This was a second failure. One thing though struck him about the proprietor. They had had a rough exchange, but yet he hadn't been dismissed on the spot. The British sense of fair play? All the same, he'd have to leave the job. Self-respect demanded it of him…

One Door Closes, Another Opens

He'd have to go to Merwanji. Tell him all that had happened, unburden his heart to him… But, on second thoughts, he felt it would be wiser to wait till he had an alternative plan of action. There were so many opportunities open to talented people in this city that had been growing fast…

There were openings in at least half a dozen newspapers and periodicals if he chose to become a journalist—Dadabhai Naoroji's *Rast Goftar*, Byramjee Malabari's *Indian Spectator* and *Voice of India*, Framji Mehta's *Kaiser-e-Hind*, Pherozeshah Mehta's *Advocate of India*, J.B. Petit's *Indian Daily Mail*... Both Indian and English language schools were opening as a result of the initiative taken by the Bombay Native Education Society way back in 1822. Teachers were in great demand. This period also saw the founding by Indians of several banks, notably the Oudh Commercial Bank in 1881, the first wholly Indian banking enterprise back then, followed by the Punjab National Bank in 1894 and the Indian Specie Bank in 1906. These banks were on the lookout for young men desirous of entering the banking profession.

But Ardeshir didn't want a job. He was looking for a vocation in the realm of manufacturing...

Ardeshir's mind was abuzz with ideas. He was totally confused and restless. He had let Merwanji down, he had betrayed his trust, and he couldn't forgive himself for that. How would he ever be able to face him again? Then, on one of his solitary evening walks, the idea hit him like a flash of lightning. He had been reading in the morning's papers about the city's police commissioner stressing the need for greater

Achievement

security measures by citizens against the increasing cases of robbery and burglary in the city. It was then that his mind hit upon the basis of all security—the lowly lock. A far cry indeed from surgical instruments, the only point of resemblance between them being that, like surgical instruments, the invention of the lock, too, went back 4000 years…

With his usual thoroughness, Ardeshir examined the locks, foreign and Indian, then available. The variety astounded him—locks which couldn't be blown open, locks where keys could be altered at will, locks which could be opened or closed by several keys but could only be unlocked by that particular key which closed them…

Most certainly, he could make better locks, locks that would guarantee absolute unpickability. Ardeshir decided it was time to call on his benefactor Merwanji again.

~

Apologizing for his inability to repay the loan immediately, he told Merwanji of all that had happened, that his instruments had impressed the chemists and that they wanted to market them but under a British name, which he could not agree.

'Of course not, I like their cheek!' was Merwanji's

only comment. After a short silence he asked a pointed question: 'But they found your instruments up to the mark?'

Ardeshir nodded.

'Then I'm proud of you. Don't be disheartened by their attitude, which I must say is most unreasonable. Somebody else does the work and they want the credit! No, you did the right thing. The important thing is, if you can manufacture surgical instruments, you can manufacture almost anything. You have the basic talent.'

Thus encouraged, Ardeshir revealed his plan to manufacture locks, better than the ones available currently in the market. Merwanji's face lit up. He was quite excited. 'You're on the right track. There's a huge demand for locks.' After a pause, 'Have you worked out how much capital you will need for this purpose?'

'I'm in the process of doing so,' Ardeshir replied. 'But, Uncle, on a matter of principle, I cannot take any more money from you until I've repaid what I already owe you.'

Merwanji let out a guffaw and then became serious. 'Don't talk about principles to me, *dikra*. My father believed, and so do I, that the greatest principle in life is to extend a helping hand to the deserving. So work out the figures and tell me. I'm interested.'

[Ardeshir] had thoroughly studied the locks

made in India. In his opinion they were crude in manufacture and offered doubtful security...

'My idea,' Ardeshir replied, 'is to band together a small group of skilled workers from Gujarat and Malabar. And, yes, I have found a place next to the Bombay Gas Works at Lalbaug. The great advantage of this place is that it leaves room for future expansion. The rent too is affordable.'

'...I'm prepared to invest a few thousands to get you started... Tell me, are there other lock-makers in our community? Or, are you the first?'

'I don't know whether I'm the first or not, but certainly I'm determined, with the help of a benefactor like you, to be the best.'

Study the Competition and Innovate

Ardeshir realized, like a true businessman, the importance of knowing his competitors, their products as well as their processes of production. He realized that the locks being made by lockmakers scattered in centres like Aligarh, Howrah, and elsewhere compared unfavourably with the imported variety. Made mostly by hand, they were crude and the technique was labour-intensive...

It didn't take Ardeshir long to train his workers in the use of implements instead of their hands. Actual production began on 7 May, 1897.

Ardeshir Godrej

It was to prove to be a historic date for the Godrej family enterprise.

Characteristically, taking on the most intricate job first and leaving the comparatively easy ones for afterwards, Ardeshir began with the manufacture of high security locks, which he named Anchor Brand...

How Ardeshir's extremely security-conscious mind worked was seen in several ingenious improvements he devised to make his locks 'absolutely unpickable'. First, he cleared several misconceptions in the public mind regarding unpickability. He warned potential buyers that the price of a lock did not depend solely on the number of levers...

Then, again, he reversed the usual process of making the locks first and then fitting the keys into them: he demonstrated the advantage of deep-forging and machine-cutting the keys, and then making the locks to fit the keys to ensure total unpickability. It took a couple of years to put on the market the highly skilled tamper-proof locks...

~

The Godrej locks effected a marked improvement even on imported locks. In all locks made hitherto, whether European or American, the levers depended for their proper working on springs attached to them.

Such locks were liable to give trouble or totally refuse to yield to the key when the levers sometimes stuck to one another, or when one of the numerous springs broke. Ardeshir was the first to invent and put on the market a lever lock without springs. Hitherto, many users had sometimes encountered a lock that defied all efforts of the skilled lock-maker to open it, leaving them no choice but to break open a valuable safe or strongroom. Even the best safe-makers' products were not free from being liable to such mishaps. The Godrej patented springless lock, as its name implies, had no springs attached to its levers and therefore was not subject to any such disorders. This was the earliest of the thirty-six Godrej patented inventions.

A Marketing Genius

[Ardeshir] had made a high-quality product and, come hell or high water, he was going to make every consumer he could reach realize it. All his pent-up frustration at the refusal of the chemist's concern to market his finely crafted surgical instruments, all his repressed fury found vent in his manner of advertising his locks. When certain British-owned newspapers refused to publish his advertisements claiming that his locks were 'as good as the imported variety', he took recourse to the increasing number of nationalist newspapers and periodicals to make the well-founded claim that his locks were 'better than the imported variety'. He printed and distributed handbills by the thousands to make as many citizens as possible in Bombay, and later in the major cities, aware of this new wonder lock that looked good and performed better...

In a small booklet that he published and distributed... Ardeshir claimed that 'the work is done on modern methods, with the aid of modern machinery with which the factory is equipped throughout at a very large outlay. We do not buy our locks or any safe parts ready-made, but we manufacture all our requirements ourselves. We have a large number of specially trained lock-makers having over 15 years' practice. This enables us to make our locks as accurately as those by the best European makers. Our keys are all deep-forged and machine-cut and not filed out by hand. We cut the keys first and make the locks to fit the keys. This makes our locks absolutely unpickable and ensures long wear.'

Steadfast Honesty

Ardeshir could not forget it even in the first flush of extraordinary success—return the three thousand rupees he had taken from Merwanji as a loan, years before Merwanji's investment in the locks product. He put the money in the same envelope Merwanji had given him, which he had carefully preserved...

Ardeshir approached him and held out the envelope. Merwanji just looked at it but he did not take it.

'Come, come, sit down,' he told Ardeshir. 'I've heard of your success. It's made me so very happy. Tell me, what are your future plans?'

'I've bought over the vacant space around the workshop. I've had to send for many more workers from Gujarat and Malabar. You won't believe it, I can hardly believe it myself, I'm building a factory in the real sense of the word. My plan is to start manufacturing safes. In fact I'm going abroad to study safe-making, particularly in London and Germany. But before leaving I've come to return the money you so kindly gave me.' He held out the envelope again. Merwanji shook his head.

'Let me confess something, *dikra*. I never meant this to be a loan. I was investing in your success. As I told you, I had complete faith in you. This was my contribution to that success.'

Ardeshir, deeply moved... was about to protest when Merwanji raised his hand...

'Listen to me. This paltry amount has come back to me manifold through my investment in your project...

Ardeshir Godrej

You won't deprive me of the joy I feel in contributing to your success, will you now?'

Ardeshir remained silent.

From Locks to Safes

[Ardeshir] was more than convinced that so far as security equipment was concerned, India's rulers could be beaten at their own game by Indians. At the same time he admitted to himself that the battle would be long and difficult and that he had still a lot to learn, particularly in the sphere of marketing...

He studied and observed and made mental notes, which he put down on paper every evening before retiring. Shrewdly, he laid his finger on certain weaknesses of the foreign safes bearing the names of well-known manufacturers. He had noticed the same weaknesses in the safes being sold in India. Inside him, he knew that these weaknesses, which affected the very concept of security, could be removed...

Finding faults was easy. Removing these, improving upon them, was a thorough test of one's mettle. Ardeshir made hundreds of designs on paper, held innumerable, interminable discussions with his engineers and *mistris*. In this paroxysm of creativity, he was like a man possessed, obsessed, totally unlike his usual calm, reticent, dignified self...

Then at last he got it. To his inventive mind it seemed so simple, so obvious that he was surprised it took so long. The sixteen-corner bend was part of the answer—one single sheet folded to form the four sides of the safe. This sheet would have sixteen bends, with the back plate welded and the door fitted subsequently. Unlike foreign safes, this simple expedient gave extra rigidity to the sides of the safe...

What about the fire-resisting quality of these safes, the quality of retaining efficiency not for a short period, but indefinitely? Here, too, Ardeshir established standards higher than those of his competitors, Indian or foreign—the ingredients should not react chemically with one another; they should have no corrosive action on iron or steel... Significantly, no other safe-maker had the courage to submit his mixture to such chemical tests. Prof. Shanial, MA, Professor of Chemistry, Queen's College, Banaras, after a prolonged examination of the mixture prepared by Ardeshir, reported that it satisfactorily fulfilled all these conditions. Ardeshir was awarded the highest prize in this regard.

Guerilla Marketing in Early Twentieth Century

Godrej safes were widely advertised under the slogan: 'A Godrej Safe in Every Home'... But Ardeshir was not satisfied with mere advertising. He went on to do something no other safe-maker in the country and, perhaps, the world had dared to do—hold a public demonstration to prove beyond a shadow of doubt the supreme fire-resisting quality of Godrej safes.

An elaborate test was conducted in the presence of John Wallace, CE, Editor of the *Indian Textile Journal*. The safe was placed in an open space adjoining the Godrej factory. Mr Wallace put into the safe a strip of pinewood to which were attached pieces of linen, calico, flannel and silk; also a small coil of pure tin electric fuse-wire, a ten-rupee currency note, a sheet of foolscap paper, several newspapers and a wooden box lacquered on the exterior and containing a piece of wax.

A fire was lit all around the safe till the outer plate became red hot. A pile of red-hot embers was put on the top so that five of the six sides were exposed to the fire. After almost four hours the safe was sluiced with buckets of water which produced the effect of a fire-hose.

On opening the safe, it was found that neither the strip of pinewood nor the tin fuse-wire showed any sign of having been affected by the heat. Except for a slight discolouration, the textile samples were unharmed, as also was the ten-rupee note…

∼

Achievement

Obviously a good safe-maker makes a good safe-breaker as well. Difficult to believe, Ardeshir had to take to safe-breaking in the course of duty and to make a point. Such an occasion arose when he had to point out to an acquaintance of his, Dhunjibhoy Batliwalla, a wealthy mill agent of Bombay, the defects he had observed in foreign safes marketed in India by well-known safe manufacturers. Batliwalla was sceptical, claiming that he had a European safe whose security had been guaranteed by its maker, it had cost him quite a bit and he had had no reason to doubt the manufacturer's claim. Ardeshir expressed a desire to have a look at the safe. Batliwalla invited him to his office, which Ardeshir visited the very next day carrying a small tool box with him—just in case. As he was examining the safe, its proud owner taunted him that if he could break it open, he would pay him whatever he asked for.

Ardeshir looked up and asked him whether he meant what he said. Batliwalla nodded, of course, and called a staff as witness to the wager. Without a word, Ardeshir removed his *pheta* and *dugla*, took out some tools and set to work. In three minutes flat, before Batliwalla's astonished, disbelieving eyes, the safe was broken open, its contents exposed. 'My God,' he exclaimed, visibly shaken. But he remained true to his word. He told Ardeshir to state the amount and he'd pay it there and then.

Ardeshir shook his head. He didn't want any payment. He wanted to teach Batliwalla a lesson, never to make claims, even claims made by foreigners, that he hadn't personally verified. And, yes, one thing more. He'd appreciate it if, by way of amends, Batliwalla bought a Godrej safe.

Never Resting on Your Laurels

Ardeshir's most important activity, after finishing with locks and security equipment manufacture, was soap-making… Long before soap manufacture came to India, Indians were using their own cleansing agents like soapsuds for washing and gram flour for bathing purposes… But Ardeshir, obsessed as he was in the pursuit of self-reliance through the production of high quality goods, would only try something that he was confident of improving upon. In soap, as it happened, he effected not only an improvement, but an almost total transformation…

Competition with foreign soap-makers was understandably bitter, a dog-eat-dog business. It was also unequal and unfair because the foreign soap-makers were favoured by the British rulers and their counterparts in India…

ACHIEVEMENT

In 1918 Ardeshir himself came out with a washing soap bar, *Chavi Chaap*, which, unlike other washing bars in use, did not shrink out of shape and cleansed better with its rich and creamy lather...

Ardeshir went on next to experiment with the idea of making stable toilet soaps from vegetable oils instead of animal fats, as was the accepted practice in most countries since the beginning of soap manufacture. The idea came to him in a curious way. Holidaying in Mahabaleshwar he collected several bags of seeds that had fallen from the trees and on an experimental basis had the oil extracted from them. Encouraged by the huge quantity of oil that was extracted, Ardeshir with considerable foresight entered into a contract with the government to acquire a monopoly of collecting these seeds. This done he started experimenting on using the oil in the manufacture of soap. Soap experts expressed doubts whether this could be done. But Ardeshir never allowed other people's doubts to deter him from the path he had laid down for himself. The experts were proved wrong when in 1920 he produced the first toilet soap to be made purely from vegetable oils and sold commercially...

The first vegetable oil soap marketed by Ardeshir after many years of research was named No. 2. When the soap was introduced, experiments were still being conducted, and when these were completed, the resultant No. 1 soap, with a lingering rose perfume, proved to be better in more ways than one. Many people used this soap for years after it was introduced in 1922. No. 2 soap continued to be sold side by side with No. 1.

Ardeshir was once asked why he introduced the No. 2 soap first and then the No. 1. Shrewdly, showing a rare sense of marketing, he replied: 'If people find soap No. 2 good, they will believe No. 1 will be even better.'

~

There were many notable men and women in India who showered paeans of praise on Ardeshir for his soaps, Rabindranath Tagore, Dr Annie Besant, Dr M.A. Ansari and C. Rajagopalachari among them. The richest tribute came from Mahatma Gandhi. Approached by another soap-maker for his blessings, he replied: 'I hold my brother Godrej in such high regard and he is of such a charitable disposition that if your enterprise is to harm him in any way, I regret very much I cannot give you my blessings.' A facsimile of this, written in Gandhiji's own hand, in Gujarati, on a postcard, is a prized possession of the Godrej family.

Words of Wisdom to Inspire You

'Every new life is a new thing under the sun; there has never been anything just like it before, never will be again. A young man ought to get that idea about himself; he should look for the single spark of individuality that makes him different from other folks, and develop that for all he is worth. Society and schools may try to iron it out of him; their tendency is to put it all in the same mold, but I say don't let that spark be lost; it is your only real claim to importance.'
—*Henry Ford*

'A man, to succeed, must possess the necessary equanimity of temperament to conceive an idea, the capacity to form it into some tangible shape, the ingenuity to put it into practical operation, the ability to favorably impress others with its merits, and the power of will that is absolutely necessary to force it to success.'
—*Thomas A. Scott*

'Our will to act becomes vigorous in proportion to the frequency and definiteness of our actions, and the brain grows to its exercise. Then truly it implements faith. When we let a resolution or a fine emotion dissipate without results, it means more than lost opportunity; it actually retards the fulfilment of future purposes and chills sensibility. There is plenty of courage among us for the abstract but not enough for the concrete, because we allow our daily bits of bravery to evaporate.'
—*Helen Keller*

'I would venture to utter a word of caution to business men. Let them study their own affairs frankly, and face the truth. If their methods are extravagant, let them realize the facts and act accordingly. One cannot successfully go against natural tendencies, and it is folly to fail to recognize them.'
—*John D. Rockefeller*

'Success is often achieved by those who don't know that failure is inevitable.'
—*Coco Chanel*

~

'You only have to do a very few things right in your life so long as you don't do too many things wrong.'
—*Warren Buffett*

'My philosophy is that not only are you responsible for your life, but doing the best at this moment puts you in the best place for the next moment.'
—*Oprah Winfrey*

~

'We need to accept that we won't always make the right decisions, that we'll screw up royally sometimes—understanding that failure is not the opposite of success, it's part of success.'
—*Arianna Huffington*

'There is nothing that can't be done. If you can't make something, it's because you haven't tried hard enough.'
—*Sakichi Toyoda*

~

'True entrepreneurship comes only from risk-taking.'
—*Dhirubhai Ambani*

'Business opportunities are like buses;
there's always another one coming.'
—*Richard Branson*

~

'You have to be burning with an idea, or a problem,
or a wrong that you want to right. If you're not
passionate enough from the start,
you'll never stick it out.'
—*Steve Jobs*

'A man can succeed at almost anything for which he has unlimited enthusiasm.'
—*Charles Schwab*

~

'Know what work you want to do and go after it. The young man who gets ahead must decide for what he wishes to do. From his own tastes, his own enthusiasm, he must get the motive and the inspiration which are to start him on his way to a successful life.'
—*Alexander Graham Bell*

'The most courageous act is still
to think for yourself. Aloud.'
—*Coco Chanel*

~

'If you don't build your dream, someone else
will hire you to help them build theirs.'
—*Dhirubhai Ambani*

'There come to us moments in life when about some things we need no proof from without. A little voice within us tells us, "You are on the right track, move neither to your left nor right, but keep to the straight and narrow way."'
—*Mahatma Gandhi*

~

'You have the right to work; do not clamour for its fruits. Let not the fruit of action be your selfish motive.'
—The Bhagvad Gita

'If you work with determination and
with perfection, success will follow.'
—*Dhirubhai Ambani*

~

'Face the thing that seems overwhelming
and you will be surprised how
your fear will melt away.'
—*Dale Carnegie*

'Our greatest glory is not in never falling,
but in rising every time we fall.'
—*Confucius*

~

'If the Sun and Moon should doubt,
They'd immediately go out.'
—*William Blake*

'The way to defeat fear: decide on a course of conduct and follow it. Keep so busy and work so hard that you forget about being afraid.'
—*Dale Carnegie*

~

'When I can't handle events,
I let them handle themselves.'
—*Henry Ford*

'He that loses money loses little,
he that loses health loses much,
but he that loses courage loses all.'
—*Anonymous*

~

'Our fears are always more
numerous than our dangers.'
—*Seneca*

'Develop success from failures. Discouragement and failure are two of the surest stepping stones to success. No other element can do so much for a man if he is willing to study them and make capital out of them. Look backward. Can't you see where your failures have helped you?
—*Dale Carnegie*

~

'Keep trying to find a differentiated model, don't just try to do what others are doing... That's where innovation comes.'
—*Kiran Mazumdar-Shaw*

'Whatever you do, be different—that was the advice my mother gave me, and I can't think of better advice for an entrepreneur. If you're different, you will stand out.'
—*Anita Roddick*

~

'In order to be irreplaceable one must always be different.'
—Coco Chanel

'There is nothing like a concrete life plan
to weigh you down. Because if you always have one
eye on some future goal, you stop paying attention
to the job at hand, miss opportunities that might
arise, and stay fixedly on one path, even when a
better, newer course might have opened up.'
—Indra K. Nooyi

~

'Don't limit yourself. Many people limit themselves
to what they think they can do. You can go as far as
your mind lets you. What you believe,
remember, you can achieve.'
—Mary Kay Ash

www.ingramcontent.com/pod-product-compliance
Lightning Source LLC
Chambersburg PA
CBHW052050220426
43663CB00012B/2515